iPad™ for the Older and Wiser

iPad™ for the Older and Wiser

Get up and running safely and quickly with the Apple iPad

Sean McManus

A John Wiley and Sons, Ltd, Publication

A John Wiley and Sons, Ltd, Publication
This edition first published 2011

Registered office
John Wiley & Sons Ltd, The Atrium, Southern Gate, Chichester, West Sussex, PO19 8SQ, United Kingdom

For details of our global editorial offices, for customer services and for information about how to apply for permission to reuse the copyright material in this book please see our website at www.wiley.com.

Reprinted Dec 2011

A catalogue record for this book is available from the British Library.

ISBN 978-1-119-97536-6

Set in Optima LT Std Roman by Melanee Habig
Printed in the U.K. by Bell & Bain

Dedication

To Karen

Acknowledgements

Thank you, as always, to my wife Karen for all her support while I was writing this book.

I've had the support of a great team at Wiley on this book, including Grace Fairley, Ellie Scott, Birgit Gruber, Chris Katsaropoulos, Chris Webb, Kate Parrett, Steve Long, Sara Shlaer and Melanee Habig. Jean Judge gave valuable feedback on behalf of the U3A.

For help with research, testing things and mocking up screenshots, thanks also to Kim Gilmour, Mark Turner, Neil Cossar, Wylda Holland, Marcus Dawson, Mark Young, Robert Kealey and Peter Döring.

About the Author

Sean McManus is an expert technology and business author. His previous books include *Microsoft Office for the Older and Wiser*, *Social Networking for the Older and Wiser* and *Web Design in Easy Steps*. His tutorials and articles have appeared in magazines including *Internet Magazine*, *Internet Works*, *Business 2.0*, *Making Music*, *Melody Maker* and *Personal Computer World*. He created Wild Mood Swings (**www.wildmoodswings.co.uk**), a web toy that shows you websites to match your mood, and has a personal website at **www.sean.co.uk**.

The Third Age Trust

The Third Age Trust is the body which represents all U3As in the UK. The U3A movement is made up of over 800 self-governing groups of older men and women who organise for themselves activities which may be educational, recreational or social in kind. Calling on their own experience and knowledge they demand no qualifications nor do they offer any. The movement has grown at a remarkable pace and offers opportunities to thousands of people to demonstrate their own worth to one another and to the community. Their interests are astonishingly varied but the members all value the opportunity to share experiences and learning with like-minded people. The Third Age Trust's endorsement of the Older and Wiser series hints at some of that width of interest.

THE THIRD AGE TRUST

THE UNIVERSITY OF THE THIRD AGE

Icons used in this book

Throughout this book, we've used icons to help focus your attention on certain information. This is what they mean:

 Equipment needed — Lets you know in advance the equipment you will need to hand as you progress through the chapter.

 Skills needed — Placed at the beginning of each chapter to help identify the skills you'll need for the chapter ahead.

 Tip — Tips and suggestions to help make life easier.

 Note — Take note of these little extras to avoid confusion.

 Warning — Read carefully; a few things could go wrong at this point.

 Try It — Go on, enjoy yourself; you won't break it.

 Trivia — A little bit of fun to bring a smile to your face.

 Summary — A short recap at the end of each chapter.

 Brain Training — Test what you've learned from the chapter.

Publisher's Acknowledgements

Some of the people who helped bring this book to market include the following:

Editorial and Production
VP Consumer and Technology Publishing Director: Michelle Leete
Associate Director – Book Content Management: Martin Tribe
Associate Publisher: Chris Webb
Executive Commissioning Editor: Birgit Gruber
Assistant Editor: Ellie Scott
Senior Project Editor: Sara Shlaer
Editorial Manager: Jodi Jensen
Editorial Assistant: Leslie Saxman
Development Editor: Grace Fairley
Technical Editor: Jean Judge
Copy Editor: Grace Fairley

Marketing
Associate Marketing Director: Louise Breinholt
Marketing Executive: Kate Parrett

Composition Services
Compositor: Melanee Habig
Proofreader: Susan Hobbs
Indexer: Potomac Indexing, LLC

Contents

PRACTICE MAKES
PERFECT

To build upon the lessons learnt in this book, visit www.pcwisdom.co.uk

- **More training tutorials**

- **Links to resources**

- **Advice through frequently asked questions**

- **Social networking tips**

- **Videos and podcasts from the author**

- **Author blogs**

Introduction

Equipment needed: Just this book, and your iPad if you already have it.

Skills needed: Some curiosity about the iPad and what it can do for you.

What is the iPad?

The iPad (see Figure 0.1) is a new type of portable computer, made by Apple. It is based on a touchscreen, which means the screen can detect when you're touching it so you don't need any other input devices. Instead of using a mouse to move a cursor around, you use your finger to touch what you want on the display screen. Rather than typing on an actual keyboard, you touch the keys on a picture of a keyboard on the screen. You slide your fingers across the screen to move items around and use a host of other 'gestures', or finger movements, to issue commands. It's a completely different way of working and having fun. Like driving a car, it takes a little time to learn the controls but before too long you are able to control it without thinking about it.

The iPad is ideal for older and wiser computer users for a few reasons. Firstly, it includes all the software you need for using the web, emailing, browsing photos, watching videos, listening to music, managing your address book, taking notes and viewing maps. That covers pretty much everything you're likely to want to do often with a computer. On top of that, it's extremely lightweight, so you can use it comfortably anywhere. The screen is easy to see, and you can magnify websites and photos to get a clearer view. The size of the screen also means the icons are well spaced out, so it's easy to control the device by touch. The iPad can be enhanced with free or cheap software applications covering virtually any hobby or interest you might have taken up in retirement, and Apple makes it easy for you to find and install these, as you'll see.

The iPad is ideal for relaxing on the sofa or for taking out and about with you. At about 9.5 inches long by 7.5 inches wide, it easily fits in your bag. Depending on what you're doing with it, Apple says you can use the iPad for up to 10 hours before you have to find a plug socket to recharge its battery. The device even includes satellite positioning and maps so you can use it to navigate in the car (from the passenger seat, of course!).

The iPad is one of many touchscreen devices that are known as tablet computers. Its slick design has inspired the market like no other, though. The iPad was first launched in April 2010 and it took just a month to sell a million of them – plus 1.5 million books to read using it and 12 million programs to run on it (called 'apps'). In the first 80 days, three million iPads were sold and more than 11,000 new software applications were created especially for the iPad.

The iPad is also compatible with most of the 225,000 software applications created for the iPod Touch and the iPhone, Apple's pocket-sized touchscreen devices.

The iPad and the iPod are not the same thing. The iPod is a pocket-sized device, originally for playing music. The iPod Touch has many of the same functions as the iPad but is much smaller.

There's more than one version of the iPad. When Apple released the second generation of the iPad (known as the iPad 2), it introduced a few new features. Two cameras were added, one on the front and one on the back. If you have an iPad with cameras, you'll learn how to use them to take pictures in Chapter 11 and how to use them for video calling in Chapter 6. The newer iPad also featured a Smart Cover (sold separately), which folds up into a stand so your iPad rests at a comfortable angle for typing or for watching the screen. When you close the cover over the screen, the iPad switches off.

If you have an original first generation iPad, you can still use nearly all the features described in this book, including the software for viewing photos. I'll let you know if there's a significant difference between your device and the newer versions as we go through the book.

Figure 0.1

Some people might be worried about the iPad because it's so completely different to what they're used to. If that sounds like you, the good news is that the iPad is much simpler to use than a desktop computer. Apple has a reputation for creating devices that are quick to learn and intuitive to use, and this book will introduce you to the important features so that you can get started quickly.

You soon learn to love the flexibility and immediacy of the iPad. It can be taken anywhere, and it wakes up from its sleep mode immediately so you can use it on impulse when you think of something you want to email, Google or watch. Most of the time, you'll find the iPad does exactly what you want, with much less fuss than the typical computer.

What computer and software will you need?

Most people use their iPads as companion devices to their main computer. You have to connect your iPad to a computer to set it up, but they are lifelong natural partners too. The iPad has much less storage space for your files than a desktop computer, but you can use your computer to back up the photos and other files on your iPad, and to swap around the films, music, books and photos stored on it.

While the iPad can do most things you'll want to do (including – with the addition of appropriate software – word processing, presentations and spreadsheets), you might want to switch back to the desktop computer to do some things from time to time.

You can use a laptop computer instead of a desktop computer to manage your iPad. I'll assume you're using a desktop computer but if you're using a laptop or other compatible computer the processes, requirements and software will be the same.

You can also synchronise your iPad with your desktop computer so that it automatically imports your contacts, browser bookmarks or photos to your iPad. That makes the iPad the ideal way to carry these things around if you already use your computer for managing your address book or photos, or if you have invested time in bookmarking all your favourite websites. The iPad has no CD drive but if you want to listen to music on it, you use your computer to copy your music CDs onto your iPad, too.

The iPad is designed to make it easy for people to use the Internet. The easiest way to get online with it is at home, if you have an Internet connection and a wireless network (Wi-Fi) set up there. If you do, it won't cost you anything extra to use your iPad at home. When you buy a broadband subscription to enable you to get fast Internet access, you will often be given a free wireless router that you can use to connect your iPad (and your computer) to the Internet. If you don't have an Internet connection at home, however, you can still surf the Internet by using 3G instead (see Chapter 1).

The software that Apple provides for managing your iPad and its content is called iTunes. To use it on a Windows computer, you need to be running Windows XP (with the free Service Pack 2 update installed), Windows Vista or Windows 7.

When your computer starts up, the title screen will tell you which version of Windows you have.

Some features, such playing high definition video on your computer, require a more modern processor, but you could just choose not to use those features if your computer isn't up to the job. They'll still work on your iPad. Generally speaking, if you bought your PC new in the last few years, it will be fine for iTunes. If your machine is older than that, check the minimum specification at **www.itunes.com/download**.

You can find out the specification of your computer by clicking the Start button, choosing Control Panel and then choosing System. This shows you the processor, RAM and Windows edition you have. A good retailer should be able to use this information to advise you whether you can use iTunes (and by extension, the iPad) with your computer.

If you use a Mac, you need to be using Mac OS X 10.5 (Leopard), released in 2007, or later. As with Windows PCs, the full specs are on the iTunes website and you should be fine if you bought your computer in the last few years.

Your computer needs to have a USB 2.0 port on it so you can connect the iPad to it. If your computer meets the other specifications, it will almost certainly have several compatible USB ports on it.

In this book, I'll be using a PC running Windows 7. If you have a different version of Windows or use a Mac, your screens might look a bit different but the process will be unaffected.

How this book is structured

This book takes you through the whole process of discovering the iPad. It's divided into four parts:

● Part I is about getting started with your iPad. You'll learn about the different iPad versions you can choose from, how to buy it and how to set it up. You'll also learn how to use your first app to keep notes and how to navigate the iPad's apps and settings.

- Part II is all about using your iPad for communications. The iPad is ideal for activities such as web browsing and emailing, and also has a great address book and diary function. I'll also show you how to view maps on your iPad. If you have an iPad with built-in cameras, you'll learn how to conduct video calls.

- Part III is about consuming various types of media on your iPad: movies, music, maps and more. You'll learn how to buy music and videos from Apple's iTunes Store, how to watch films and listen to music, and how to copy your music CDs into your iPad. In this part, you'll also discover how to create playlists of your favourite songs.

- Part IV shows you how to have fun with the iPad, downloading games and other types of apps, as well as books to read on your iPad. If you have an iPad with cameras, this part of the book will show you how to take photos and shoot videos using your iPad too. Whichever iPad version you have, you'll learn how to view your photos on your iPad.

As you work through the book, you'll build on some of the skills that you learned earlier on. I recommend you read the book in the order in which it's written, but I'll provide reminders and cross-references as appropriate, for those who prefer to jump around the chapters. There is also a glossary and an index you can use to refer back to anything you might have missed or forgotten.

Visit www.pcwisdom.co.uk or www.sean.co.uk to download a free bonus chapter, with detail of some of the new iPad features Apple has introduced since this book was published.

PART I
Getting Started with Your iPad

Writing notes on this is a piece of cake.
—All you need is a fine magic marker.

Choosing and buying your iPad

1

Equipment needed: A credit card!

Skills needed: None, but computer-buying experience might make this easier for you.

Once you've decided to buy an iPad, you have a few more decisions to make. There are several different versions of the iPad, and where you can buy it will depend on which version you want to get.

The two main decisions you need to make are: how much storage space you need; and how you want to connect to the Internet (by using Wi-Fi only, or by using 3G as well). In this chapter, I'll talk you through these choices.

How much storage space do you need?

You can't add extra storage space to your iPad later, in the way you can add space to a desktop computer by connecting a new hard drive or other storage device, so before you buy your iPad you need to decide how much space you're going to need.

The iPad is available with three different capacities: 16GB, 32GB and 64GB. (GB is short for gigabyte, a unit for measuring how much information fits on a device or disk.) How much is that? Well, one gigabyte is enough for about 10 hours of music bought from iTunes or an hour of film (half that if it's high definition). You'll get about 220 songs to a gigabyte if you copy your own CDs using the Good Quality setting (which is lower quality than iTunes downloads, but good enough for small speakers). My 7 megapixel digital camera gets about 400 photos to a gigabyte, but your camera might have larger or smaller files depending on whether it has a higher resolution (for example, 12 megapixels) or lower. Books vary greatly in size; you might get about 350 text-only books (including novels) or just 40 illustrated books to a gigabyte. These are all just rules of thumb. You'll get a lot fewer songs to a gigabyte if you're into prog rock songs with 13-minute guitar solos, for example.

The storage space is also used up by apps, which vary greatly in size from negligibly small up to about a third of a gigabyte for those that are rich in sound and images. If you want to put any books or other documents on your iPad, these will be drawing on the same pool of storage space, too.

Apple uses some of the storage space for its own software, so there is less space for you to use than the advertised device capacity. A 16GB iPad only has 14GB you can use, for example. Don't buy an iPad with just enough space. Leave room for Apple's software – and for your music or photo collection to grow.

It's not hard to see how the space can fill up after you've used the iPad for a while, especially if you want to download lots of films. A 16GB iPad might have enough space for three films, a few large apps and lots of small ones, 40 CDs of music, and a few hundred photos. A desktop computer costing about the same as an iPad might have ten or more times as much storage space, so there's less space on the iPad than you're used to having.

That said, it's important to remember that you can change the music, videos, apps and photos on your iPad regularly. It isn't designed to store all of your files all of the time. You'll typically store your films, music and photos on your computer, and copy them to your iPad when you want to use them. You might change the films or TV programmes when you've watched those that are currently on your iPad, or put new music on and take some old music off when you fancy a change.

If you already have a music or photo collection on your computer that will fit on one of the higher capacity iPads, you might want to buy one of those. You'll pay more for the higher capacity devices, but they are priced so that the increased capacity is a relatively small investment. At the time of writing, you can double your storage space from 16GB to 32GB by spending 20% more on your iPad. I bet a lot of people have been seduced by Apple's pricing into buying a bigger capacity iPad than they originally planned to. You can justify splashing out more because it will save you time moving files around later, particularly if you're a movie buff and you want to carry your favourite films wherever you go.

If you don't already have a music or photo collection on your PC that you want to be able to store in its entirety on the iPad, you might well find that 16GB is enough for your needs. Some people never fill that, and activities like watching YouTube videos, emailing and using the web have little or no impact on your storage space.

Connecting to the Internet: Wi-Fi or 3G?

There are two different types of Internet connection that the iPad can support: Wi-Fi and 3G. All iPads can use Wi-Fi. This is a way of connecting to the Internet wirelessly that works in a small area, such as in an Internet café, or in your own home if you have a Wi-Fi router for your broadband connection. It's usually free for you to connect to public Wi-Fi, but places like hotels sometimes charge for access. Wi-Fi has the advantage of being faster than 3G, but the drawback of only being available in some areas, and in a fairly small radius in those areas.

There is also a version of the iPad that supports 3G communications, which is a type of mobile communications (3G is short for 'third generation mobile communications'). It works a bit like a mobile phone in that you can connect anywhere you can get a mobile signal, but you have to buy a 3G data plan (basically, a contract) from a mobile phone company to be allowed to use their network. Note that although you'll buy your data plan from a mobile phone company, the iPad isn't designed to support voice calling.

You have a free choice of companies you can buy your 3G data plan from, but not all mobile phone companies support the iPad. At the time of writing, in the UK you can get a contract from O2, Three, Orange or Vodafone.

Unlike with a mobile phone, you don't need to have a long-term contract. While many of the contracts re-bill automatically at the end of each month, you can typically cancel at any time and start up again later. You might just want to buy a month's 3G access for your summer holiday and then cancel it when you return, for example. Daily and weekly contracts are also available, so you don't have to buy a full month's worth of access.

The contracts allow you to download a certain amount of data over the 3G network within a certain timeframe. O2, for example, offers a contract that gives you 1GB of data to download within 30 days, which amounts to about 200 songs, two hours of video or 10,000 web pages (according to O2's own estimates).

Data just means information. It includes maps, web page content, music, videos and anything else you get from the Internet.

The 3G contracts sometimes provide free access to subscription-based public Wi-Fi hotspots too. This can help your data allowance to go further because you can download as much as you like over Wi-Fi, in public or at home. It's only the content downloaded using the 3G connection that's restricted.

When you sign up with a 3G provider, they will send you a micro SIM card to insert into your iPad. This is a different size to the SIM cards used in mobile phones. Some of the 3G providers require you to sign up on the web (such as Three and Orange), and others will enable you to sign up directly on your iPad (O2 and Vodafone). See Chapter 2 for advice on using your micro SIM card.

Check the Apple website for the latest data plans and providers. You can find links to information like this on this book's section of my website at **www.sean.co.uk**.

The 3G iPad also has GPS, a positioning system that uses a network of satellites to work out where you are. If you want to use maps extensively, this can be extremely useful, although there are more basic (and less accurate) positioning features in the Wi-Fi iPad too.

Whether you need a Wi-Fi-only iPad or one that also supports 3G will depend on how you intend to use it. If you want to use your iPad mainly at home and you have a Wi-Fi router at home, then the Wi-Fi version will be perfect. Most of its features will work wherever you are, but you won't be able to download new content from the Internet or from the iTunes store unless you connect to a Wi-Fi network. You'll have fast Internet access through your own Wi-Fi connection while at home, and will also be able to connect to the Internet at many big name and independent cafes all over the world.

If you want to ensure you can connect to the Internet from almost anywhere (depending on the availability of the 3G network), then the 3G iPad might be for you. It costs more than the Wi-Fi version to buy, however, and you'll have to pay additionally for access to the 3G network. The 3G iPad is the natural choice for somebody who travels a lot, especially within the UK, or for someone who wants to make extensive use of the maps feature on the road. It might be expensive to use 3G roaming abroad, although you might be able to buy a data plan in the country you are visiting to cut the cost.

If you do opt for a 3G iPad, it will use Wi-Fi instead wherever that is available, to save you using up your data allowance unnecessarily.

Buying accessories for your iPad

There are a number of accessories you can buy for the iPad, some made by Apple and some made by other companies. If you buy your iPad from a shop, you'll probably be offered one or more of the following:

- **iPad dock:** A stand for your iPad that keeps it upright while it charges. This isn't essential, and seems expensive if the main benefit is to keep your desk tidy while the iPad charges.

- **iPad keyboard dock:** A full-size keyboard that you can plug your iPad into so it stands up, like a monitor screen. You can also charge your iPad while it's in the dock. If you typically use a keyboard-based PC, you might be tempted to get one of these straight away, but don't buy one until you've tried the iPad's on-screen keyboard. You probably won't need to add a real keyboard. Few people do.

- **iPad USB power adapter:** You get one of these with your iPad anyway, but you could buy another so you've got one for the office and one for the home. If you buy an extra one it has a 6m cable on it, so if your tables are bizarrely distant from your plug sockets, this might come in handy.

- **iPad Camera Connection Kit:** This enables you to copy photos directly from your camera or its SD card (memory card) into the iPad. This is a useful accessory to take on holiday, so you can email photos from your iPad and view slideshows on it even when you don't have access to your computer to copy them across.

- **iPad case:** A case helps to protect your iPad. These are made by many companies but I recommend Apple's own cases, which also enable you to stand your iPad up for use as a picture frame or TV screen, or lay it on the desk at an angle that's comfortable for typing. Apple's Smart Cover also turns the iPad off when the screen is covered and starts it up again when it's opened, but it's not compatible with the first generation iPad (the one without cameras) and it doesn't protect the back of the device.

- **Screen protector:** These are plastic films you can apply to the surface of your iPad to prevent scratching. They can be hard to apply without getting air bubbles trapped between the screen protector and the screen. Apple doesn't sell screen protectors, perhaps because it believes you don't need one.

- **Cleaning cloths:** You don't need any special cloth to keep your iPad clean. You can use a glasses cleaning cloth (available cheaply from opticians).

- **Printer:** Apple uses a wireless technology it calls AirPrint, which enables your iPad to send documents to a compatible printer. Unless you plan to do a lot of printing from your iPad, I wouldn't worry about getting a printer for it. You could just send documents to your main computer and print them from there. When you next replace your printer, look out for one that also supports AirPrint, though.

- **Extended warranty/insurance:** Apple offers a one-year warranty with the iPad but you can buy an extended warranty if you want to. If you want to insure your iPad against accidental damage while in transit, you can often have it covered more cheaply under your home contents insurance policy.

You don't have to buy any of these, although the iPad case is a good investment, and the Camera Connection Kit is useful for holiday photo fun. If you find you have money burning a hole in your pocket, it's probably better to buy a larger capacity iPad than to stock up on accessories.

Where to buy your iPad

The iPad is a hot gadget, so lots of shops want to stock it. There's probably somewhere near you that sells it, and where you might even have the opportunity to try it out before you buy.

Apple has its own shops in major cities and towns, where you can get expert consultancy on your purchase. The store usually has Apple devices set up that you can just go in and play with, so it's the perfect place to get a feel for the device before making your decision. The team in the store can also pre-install a 3G micro SIM card for you if you want, which will save you a slightly fiddly job later (see Chapter 2). You might also be able to get your iPad set up for you in the store, so you don't have to connect your iPad to your computer before you start using it (see Chapter 2).

Apple also sells online (with free engraving available) and by phone. Visit **www.apple.com** for store details, the phone number and online shopping. The downside of buying direct from Apple is that you won't get a discount, because Apple won't want to compete unfairly with its retail partners.

Other consumer electronics stores and mobile phone stores also sell the iPad. Mobile phone stores might only sell the 3G version with a contract, so if you want a Wi-Fi version it's best to look elsewhere. If you do buy from a mobile phone shop on a contract, study the small print. The iPad will often be heavily discounted, but that's because you sign a contract to pay a monthly 3G fee for two years. Those deals work out well for business travellers who use their iPad heavily, but probably won't be ideal for someone who will mostly use their iPad at home or other places where Wi-Fi is available. As I said before, you can use a 3G iPad and just pay for a month or so of 3G access when you're on holiday, so you don't have to sign a contract and pay every month.

Major online retailers, including Amazon, also sell the iPad and their prices are sometimes cheaper than those typically found in the high street.

Summary

- The iPad is available with capacities of 16GB, 32GB and 64GB.

- You can't upgrade the memory of your iPad later, so make sure you pick one that's big enough now.

- You can use your computer to swap around the files on your iPad easily, so it doesn't matter if they don't all fit at once.

- All iPads can use free Wi-Fi to connect to the Internet, including through your wireless router at home if you have one.

- Some iPads also enable 3G communications. You have to pay more to buy a 3G device, and have to pay for using the 3G network.

- Wi-Fi offers a connection within a small area, such as in a café or in your home. 3G is more like the connection for a mobile phone and can be used wherever there is a 3G signal.

- You can buy your iPad direct from Apple, from a mobile communications company or from a consumer electronics store.

- There are lots of accessories you can buy for the iPad. A good case will protect it and enable it to stand up for viewing.

- The Camera Connection Kit enables you to copy photos to your iPad so you can email them to people while you're still on holiday.

Brain training

At the end of each chapter of this book, there's a short quiz to refresh the points covered and give you a break before the next chapter. Sometimes there's more than one right answer.

1. Wi-Fi is:

(a) A wireless Internet connection

(b) A companion for Hus-Bandi

(c) A type of mobile phone

(d) A high tech way to order coffee

2. A 3G iPad is:

(a) One that is moving incredibly fast

(b) One that costs £3,000

(c) One that can use a mobile communications network to access the Internet

(d) One that weighs the same as a few paperclips

3. To store the most films, music, photos and apps on your iPad, you need one with:

(a) 16GB

(b) 32GB

(c) 64GB

(d) 3G

4. AirPrint is:

(a) A way of printing from the iPad on a compatible printer

(b) Where the Red Arrows write words in the sky

(c) A special printing effect used on the iPad box

(d) A way of sending content to your iPad

5. You can use the iPad Smart Cover to:

(a) Turn off your iPad

(b) Prop up your iPad to watch videos on it

(c) Prop up your iPad for typing

(d) Protect the back of your iPad

Answers

Q1 – a   Q2 – c   Q3 – c   Q4 – a   Q5 – a, b and c

Setting up your iPad

2

Equipment needed: An iPad and a computer capable of running iTunes (see the Introduction to this book), with a connection to the Internet. Ideally, a broadband Internet connection and a Wi-Fi router set up at home. A micro SIM card, if you have a 3G iPad.

Skills needed: None, but experience installing software is helpful.

You've ripped off the packaging, admired the shiny screen and you now want to start playing with your iPad. The bad news is that you need to spend a little bit of time setting it up before you can do anything with it. The good news is that – if your experience is anything like mine – it's easier to set up your iPad than it was to get it out of the shrink-wrap.

To set up your iPad, you'll need to connect it to a computer. Ideally, it should be your own computer, so that you can continue to use it to manage your iPad in future. If that's not possible, you can get away with using a friend's computer to set up your iPad. You won't be able to use a computer in the library or Internet café, though, because you'll need to install software on it, and they are usually restricted to stop people doing that. If you buy your iPad from an Apple store, they might be able to set up your iPad for you in the store.

In this chapter, I'll guide you through the process of setting up your iPad. You'll also get a first glimpse at how it works, and will be able to configure it so that it's as easy to use as possible.

Downloading and installing iTunes

The software that is used to manage your iPad from your computer is called iTunes, and even if you don't have an iPad, the software is free. It enables you to manage music and video on your computer, and also provides access to Apple's store for buying music, films, and iPad software (apps). Apple installs iTunes by default on its computers, so this section only applies if you have a Windows computer. The iPad doesn't come with a software disc, so you'll need to download iTunes from Apple's website and then install it.

If you have an iPod or iPhone, you will have iTunes installed on your computer already. You don't need to install it again and can skip this section. If your version of iTunes is too old, the software will tell you and help you upgrade.

If you're not comfortable with installing software on your computer, you might want to get a friend or family member to help. It's not hard, though, and if you're familiar with using a web browser you should be fine. Here are the steps you should follow to install iTunes on your computer:

1. Open a web browser, such as Internet Explorer.

2. Into the address bar at the top of your browser (see Figure 2.1), type in **www.itunes.com/download** and press the Return key (also known as the Enter key).

Figure 2.1

3. Enter your email address into the box provided (on the left in Figure 2.2). If you don't want to receive any emails from Apple, untick the boxes. Click the Download Now button.

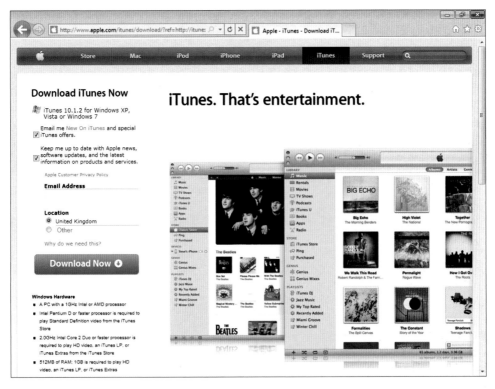

Figure 2.2

4. You can ignore the warning that Windows gives you that this program might harm your computer. As long as you've followed the steps here to download it directly from Apple, it will be safe. You will be asked whether you want to Run or Save the program. Click Run.

5. Read the option screens and click Next to advance through them. You'll need to accept the licence agreement, and decide whether to add shortcuts to your desktop (recommended) and whether to allow Apple to update the software automatically (recommended for security reasons). You can also choose whether to make iTunes the default for playing music on your computer. I don't recommend you select this until you've tried iTunes and decided you'd like to use it all the time. You can change this setting in the iTunes preferences later. Unless you want to change something, it's okay to leave the settings unchanged during installation.

6. After you click Install, put the kettle on. The installation takes several minutes. You'll see a green progress bar go from left to right many times. When the installation is complete, iTunes will tell you.

7. Restart your computer.

Companies sometimes redesign their websites and software, so the screen designs and options might differ slightly for you.

Connecting your iPad to your computer

If you've tried switching your iPad on, you'll know that it won't let you do anything until you to connect it to iTunes. Now's the time to do that, so dig out the white cable that came with your iPad.

It has a different shaped connector on each end. The long, flat plug goes into the iPad (see Figure 2.3). The opening is on the edge of the device, adjacent to the round button on its front. The plug goes in with the side with the icon to the front of the device. The other plug goes into a USB port on your computer. You'll often find USB ports on both the back and the front of your computer and it doesn't matter which one you use. You might previously have used USB ports to connect your camera, scanner or other device to your computer.

The plugs on the iPad cable will only go in one way around, so if you can't get it to fit easily, try flipping the plug over. Don't force it, or you might damage the cable or the socket.

When you connect your iPad to your PC for the first time, a box will pop up on your PC screen to say that a device driver is being installed. When the box confirms your device is ready, you can click the button with the red cross in its top right corner to close the box. An Autoplay box will also open asking you what you want to do with this device. You can ignore this box and just close it in the same way without taking any other action for now.

Figure 2.3

The iTunes software will then start on your PC. This can take a moment or two, so be patient if it doesn't appear instantly.

The process for setting up your device using iTunes will depend on which version of the iPad you're using and whether you have used any previous iPads, iPods or iPhones on this computer. From time to time Apple changes the iTunes software, too, and the features available during setup. It's easy enough to follow, though. Setup only takes a few minutes, and Apple is as keen as you are for you to get started quickly!

If you close iTunes by mistake or it doesn't open for some reason, you can restart it like any other program. If you made no changes to the default options when installing iTunes, you will have an icon on your desktop, which you can double-click. Alternatively, put your mouse cursor over the Start button in the bottom left of your computer screen, click it, click All Programs, click the iTunes folder and then click the iTunes icon.

If you have a 3G iPad, you can still use it with the Wi-Fi settings even if you don't have a 3G SIM card yet. You'll see an error message, though, and iTunes will tell you to connect your iPad to the computer again after the SIM card has been inserted (see 'Setting up a 3G connection', later in this chapter).

During setup, you will be invited to set up Find My iPad. I'll show you how to do this later, so you can skip this step for now.

To use many of the features of your iPad, you'll need to have an Apple ID; this is a combination of your email address and a password that you make up yourself. It's used for FaceTime (see Chapter 6) and to buy things like music, films and apps. Apple will ask you to create an Apple ID and will require you to enter credit card details. The iTunes store uses a secure connection, so your credit card details are safe and cannot be stolen by anyone as they go over the Internet.

You will also have to accept the iPad software licence agreement. This is mainly about the copyright in the content you download to the iPad, such as maps, and also includes clauses about what data Apple collects about you and how it uses it. You can scroll through the terms and conditions to read them, but you have to accept them to be able to use your iPad anyway. I'll flag up anything you should be aware of with regards to privacy as you discover new features in this book.

If you have another iPad, or an iPod or iPhone, you'll be asked whether you'd like to restore your device from the backup of one of your other devices. I recommend that you select the button to set this up as a new iPad and then click Continue.

During setup, iTunes will ask you to give your iPad a name (see Figure 2.4). If you're the kind of person who likes to give your car a pet name, then feel free to let your creativity run riot and dream up a fitting name for your new flat-faced friend. Mine is just called 'Sean's iPad'. If you end up being a two-iPad family (or more!), the name helps you to tell which is which.

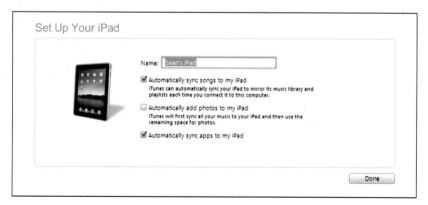

Figure 2.4

You then have three settings to choose:

- **Automatically sync songs to my iPad.** Whenever you connect your iPad to your computer, iTunes can automatically copy any new music on your computer to your iPad, or 'sync' them. This jargon is short for 'synchronisation' because the process ensures that the computer and iPad are consistent in terms of the files they hold, similar to the way that synchronised watches are in agreement about the time. The files copied to your iPad might be music you bought from the iTunes store using your computer, or that you added to your computer by inserting a music CD and copying it to your computer (called 'ripping it'). Unless you have too much music on your computer to fit the iPad, I recommend you keep this setting selected. Chapter 10 reveals the other ways you can choose music to copy from your computer to your iPad.

- **Automatically add photos to my iPad.** If there is room left over after your music has been copied to your iPad, iTunes can copy across your photos. I prefer to choose which photos go onto my iPad to make sure they are the best ones and not just those randomly chosen by iTunes, so I don't select this setting. iTunes leaves it deselected by default, too. You'll find out more about adding photos to your iPad in Chapter 11.

- **Automatically sync apps to my iPad.** You can download new software apps from the iTunes store using your computer or directly on your iPad. If you buy them on your computer, this setting will copy them automatically to your iPad. It's a good idea to leave this setting selected. You'll learn how to organise the apps on your iPad properly later (see Chapter 12) but, for now, this will ensure any apps you buy on your computer automatically get copied across.

You can change all of these settings at any time later on, so don't fret about making the right decision. For now, the defaults (yes to synchronising songs and apps, but no to synchronising photos), are fine.

Once you've selected your settings, your iPad will begin to synchronise with your computer using iTunes.

Synchronising your iPad with your computer

Each time you connect your iPad to your computer, iTunes will leap into action and automatically begin copying any new apps and music from your computer to your iPad (unless you have changed the default settings). Your iPad screen will say 'Sync in Progress' (you can cancel the sync by sliding the switch on your iPad that is usually used to unlock the device). When you sync, any content you have created or downloaded on your iPad will be backed up on your computer too.

Of course, the first time you connect to your computer, you might not have any music or other content on your computer to synchronise with the iPad. Which is good news, because it means we can hurry along to start playing with the iPad itself very soon!

Figure 2.5 shows what iTunes looks like when your iPad is connected to it. The central box at the top shows the status of iTunes, and will show you when files are being copied across. Underneath that, you can see buttons to go into the settings for Info, Apps, Music, Films, TV Programmes, Podcasts and iTunes U (see Chapter 9), Books, and Photos. Figure 2.5 indicates the buttons for these content types. To change which files of a particular content type are synchronised, such as which TV programmes are copied to the iPad, click its button and then change the settings. You'll learn how to use the settings for music, film and more in later chapters, but feel free to explore.

If you change any of the settings, you'll need to press the Apply button in the bottom right corner to make your iPad synchronise with those new settings. If you change your mind, click the Revert button in the bottom right and iTunes will ignore your changes. These buttons only appear when you change settings.

If you don't see your iPad settings in iTunes, select it in the window on the left. You'll find it listed by the name you gave it under the heading Devices, as you can see in Figure 2.5.

If you've ever spent time trying to work out how on earth you've managed to fill up your computer's hard disk, you'll love this next feature. At the bottom of the screen (see Figure 2.5), you can see a Capacity graph showing how much space is left on your iPad, and how much of each content type you have on it so far. You can see, for example, that I've got a lot of video (purple) and apps (green) on mine. If I need to clear some space off to put new content on, I can start by removing the videos I've watched (see Chapter 10) and my least favourite apps (see Chapter 12).

If the iTunes status at the top of your computer's screen says 'OK to disconnect', you can remove the plug in your iPad. If it doesn't say that, you should eject the iPad first. You'll be relieved to know this doesn't actually hurl it across the room and out of the door, but just stops the computer from trying to copy files to it. The Eject button in iTunes is beside the name of your iPad in the left hand column. Put the mouse cursor over it, and click the left mouse button. iTunes will tell you that it's OK to disconnect, and you can then remove the iPad's plug. You can also cancel a sync by dragging the slider on the iPad's screen.

If you don't want your iPad to synchronise when you connect it to the computer, connect the iPad, and then hold down the shift and control keys on your keyboard until the iPad appears in iTunes.

Figure 2.5

Charging your iPad

Your iPad will warn you when the battery gets low. The best way to charge your iPad is to connect it to the mains electricity. First, you need to assemble the plug, which comes in two parts (see Figure 2.6). The two parts slot together to create a standard three-pin plug.

The cable you used to connect your iPad to your computer can then be connected to the plug. The USB connector that previously went into the computer slots into the hole on the back of the plug (see Figure 2.7).

At the top of your iPad screen is the status bar, which includes information about your iPad and the current time. In the top right corner, you can see the battery indicator. It shows, as a percentage, how charged your battery is. When the battery is charging, the battery icon will have a lightning bolt through it.

Figure 2.6

If your computer's USB port provides enough power, the iPad can also charge slowly while it is connected to your computer. For this to work, the iPad needs to be in sleep mode and the computer needs to be switched on. If the computer is turned off or in sleep mode, the battery might drain rather than charge. Apple also warns against connecting to a USB port on your keyboard, or to a USB hub, a device that enables you to add multiple USB connections to a single USB port. By far the best approach is to use the power adapter to charge from the mains.

A fully charged battery has enough juice for most journeys, and you'll only need to charge your iPad every few days if you use it around the home. Apple claims that the battery will last for up to ten hours while using Wi-Fi, watching videos or listening to music. If you use 3G to connect to the Internet, the battery life is cut back to up to nine hours.

Figure 2.7

There are steps you can take to prolong your battery life:

● Don't leave your iPad in a hot car and keep it out of the sun. Apple says heat degrades battery performance more than anything else.

● Adjust the brightness to the minimum comfortable level (see 'Adjusting other iPad settings', later in this chapter).

● Every month, go through at least one charge cycle, charging the battery to 100% and then running it down completely.

● If your iPad gets hot when charging and you have bought a protective case for it, remove it from its case.

● Keep your iPad software updated. When you connect your iPad to iTunes, on the Summary pane there is a button to check for updates to your iPad software. Software updates might include features that help optimise battery use.

● Turn off Wi-Fi and/or 3G when you won't be using them (see later in this chapter).

● Minimise the use of location services, such as maps (you can turn off location services in the Settings app, which is covered later in this chapter).

● Turn off push notifications. You'll learn about these later, but they enable apps to alert you to new information when you're not using them (see Chapter 12).

● Download new emails and other regular updates less frequently. Check fewer email accounts automatically, and turn off features to push email to your iPad (see Chapter 5).

Since the battery wears out over time and can only be replaced by Apple, these tips will also help you to prolong the life of your whole iPad. Apple estimates that you can fully charge and discharge your iPad a thousand times before the battery performance falls below 80% of what it should be. Even if you managed to exhaust your iPad every day, that would give you nearly three years of life, so your iPad is designed to last many years.

You can charge your iPad abroad using the power adapter. You'll need to plug the three-pin plug into a travel plug adapter that fits the wall socket of the country you are visiting.

Switching on your iPad

Now it's time to start playing with your iPad. Hold your iPad so that the round button on its front surface is at the bottom. This button is called the Home button. On the top edge of the iPad, on the right, you can find the Sleep/Wake button. Press and hold the Sleep/Wake button until the Apple logo appears. After a moment or two, the screen will come to life and you will see the time at the top, and a slider at the bottom of the screen (see Figure 2.8).

The slider is the first touchscreen control you'll use. Put your finger on the arrow and move your finger to the right, keeping it in contact with the glass all the time. As you move your finger, the arrow will move with it. When it reaches the right edge of its box, release your finger and your iPad will be unlocked. The Home screen will appear showing a number of icons (see Figure 2.9).

Use the skin of your fingers, not your fingernails. It's easiest if you use the surface of your fingers where your fingerprints are. You don't have to press the screen. Just touch it.

Figure 2.8

When you're not using your iPad, there are two different states it can be in. Firstly, it can be locked (also known as sleep mode). This might be a bit surprising if you aren't expecting it but, after two minutes of inactivity, the iPad locks itself to save power. You can also force it to lock straight away by pressing the Sleep/Wake button. A locked iPad can still play music and responds to volume controls, but has the screen switched off and won't respond to your touch. To unlock the iPad, press the Home button and then use the slider. Alternatively, if you have a smart cover on your iPad (not available for the first generation iPad), just open the cover. An iPad can be unlocked almost instantly.

The other state your iPad can be in is fully switched off. You could switch off your iPad at the end of the day, although in practice people often just leave their iPad locked instead so that it will start up more quickly the next time they need it. To turn your iPad off, press and hold the Sleep/Wake button and then drag the red slider to turn it off. You turn it on again by pressing and holding the Sleep/Wake button.

The iPad remembers what you were doing before it was locked or switched off, so all your apps will be exactly where you left them. If you are halfway through an email when your plane is called for boarding, lock your iPad so you can stash it in your bag for now and continue writing later.

Changing the iPad orientation

You can use the iPad any way around. Try rotating it, and you'll see the screen contents rotate too, so that you're always looking at them the right way up. Figures 2.9 and 2.10 show the iPad in the portrait (taller than wide) and landscape (wider than tall) orientations.

As you try different activities with the iPad, you'll find some work more naturally in one orientation than the other. When writing notes or emails, I prefer to use the landscape orientation because it makes the keyboard bigger. You can also rotate the iPad to match the shape of photos (portrait or landscape), so you can see them at their maximum size (see Chapter 11).

Figure 2.9

Figure 2.10

Navigating the Home screen

Each activity on the iPad takes place within a software application called an app. On the Home screen, you can see icons for the apps that come installed on your iPad: Calendar, Contacts, Notes, Maps, Videos, YouTube, iTunes (a music and film store), App Store, Game Center, Settings, Safari, Mail, Photos and iPod (a music player). On iPads with cameras, you will also see the Camera, Photo Booth and FaceTime apps. To start an app, just touch its icon briefly and then lift your finger. A quick touch on an icon like this is called 'tapping' it.

Don't hold your finger on an icon for too long, otherwise you'll go into the mode for arranging icons (see Chapter 12). If the icons start jiggling, press the Home button on the front of your iPad to make them stop.

Try starting the apps to see what they look like. Without a web connection or content on your iPad, many of them won't do much, but you can take a quick peek and practise using the touchscreen. When you've finished exploring an app or if you get lost, press the Home button and you'll go back to the Home screen, where you can pick another app.

On a computer, you use a mouse to move the cursor to what you want and then click the mouse button to select it. As you've now discovered, on the iPad, you just tap it with your finger on the touchscreen.

Setting up your Internet connection

In this section, I'll show you how to connect to the Internet. You'll need your Wi-Fi network name and password, and your micro SIM from your 3G data provider, if you have a 3G iPad. After you've set up your web connection, to see it working, go to Chapter 7 on browsing the web or Chapter 8 on Maps.

Setting up a Wi-Fi connection

To set up a Wi-Fi connection, you will need the name of the Wi-Fi Network and its password. If you're using your own router, you can find out or change the password by checking your router settings. If you are using public Wi-Fi, you will usually be given the network name and password together. To set up a Wi-Fi connection, follow these steps:

1. Go to the Settings app (its icon shows cog wheels) by tapping it on the Home screen.

2. Press Wi-Fi, in the menu on the left. The Wi-Fi settings appear, as shown in Figure 2.11.

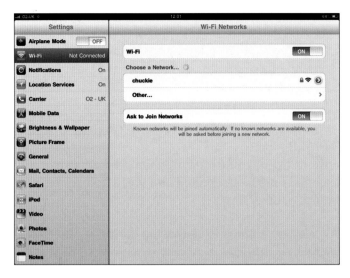

Figure 2.11

3. Make sure the switch on the right says that Wi-Fi is on. You can touch this switch and slide it left or right to turn Wi-Fi on or off. When you see switches like this, you can also just tap them to switch them on or off.

4. Choose a network to connect to by tapping its name. You might have to choose the right one (your one) from a number of these if there are several networks nearby.

5. Enter the password for the network when prompted. A keyboard will appear on the touchscreen. When you type a password, you can only see the latest character entered for a moment, so keep an eye on the characters as you type to make sure there aren't any errors. To enter a number or symbol, tap the key labelled '.?123'. You can hide the keyboard at any time by tapping the button in the bottom right of it. To bring it back, tap one of the form boxes. For more tips on using the keyboard, see Chapter 3.

6. Press the Join button on the keyboard.

7. When you are connected, a tick appears beside the name of the Wi-Fi network in the Wi-Fi settings.

After you've joined a Wi-Fi network for the first time, your iPad will join it automatically in future, without asking you for the password. That means your web browsing should be seamless from now on while you're using the same Wi-Fi network.

If you're not connected to Wi-Fi, your iPad will tell if you it comes across other Wi-Fi networks you might be able to join. You won't necessarily be able to join them, though. They might belong to your neighbours or to nearby businesses. You can stop your iPad from telling you about networks it finds by turning off the switch beside 'Ask to Join Networks' in the Wi-Fi settings.

When you type a password on a PC, it just shows up as a line of dots on screen. On the iPad, each character appears on screen for a moment to allow you to check it's correct, so whenever you enter a password, take care nobody with sharp eyes is reading it over your shoulder.

Setting up a 3G connection

To start using 3G, you need to have a micro SIM card from your 3G data plan provider. If you buy direct from Apple, the company can install the micro SIM for you. If you buy your data plan at a mobile phone shop, they might be able to install your SIM card for you there, too. Otherwise, you'll need to phone or register with a 3G provider online to get them to post you a SIM. If you receive your micro SIM by post, these are the steps you need to follow:

1. Your micro SIM card will probably come in a piece of plastic the size of a credit card. You need to snap the SIM card out of it, to fit it into your iPad. Keep a note of its mobile broadband number, which will look like a mobile phone number.

2. Use the special SIM eject tool that came with your iPad to open the SIM tray on your iPad. When you hold the iPad with the Home button at the bottom, there is a tiny round hole on the left edge. On the original iPad, it's towards the bottom, and on the iPad 2 it's near the top. If you can't find it, consult the leaflet that came with your iPad. Insert the tool (or a paperclip will do) in here, and the tray will spring out. Figure 2.12 shows the SIM tray in the side of the iPad, with the eject tool.

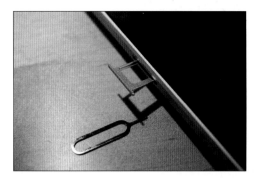

Figure 2.12

3. The tray can be completely removed from the iPad. Put the micro SIM card into the tray. It will only go in one way around. If it's too big, check whether there is any more plastic on it that is designed to be snapped off. Remember you can only use a micro SIM card, and not a standard mobile phone SIM card.

4. Carefully replace the tray.

5. When you turn the iPad on, you'll see a message telling you the iPad is waiting for the SIM to be activated.

The next steps you need to take may vary depending on which 3G provider you use. For O2, which enables you to sign up on the iPad itself, the steps are:

1. Ensure that you are using the latest version of the iPad software. Connect your iPad to iTunes on your computer and click the Check for Update button in the summary pane. Disconnect your iPad in the usual way.

2. Go into your iPad settings by tapping the Settings app icon on the Home screen.

3. Tap Mobile Data on the left and then tap View Account on the right.

4. Touch each box in turn on the form (see Figure 2.13), and the keyboard will appear so you can enter the information required. Enter your first and last names. The telephone box, confusingly, is not for your phone number. It's for the mobile broadband number that came with your SIM card. You also need to invent a password and enter it twice (to make sure you type it correctly). When you finish entering information in one box, tap the next box on the screen. To scroll the form, touch it and drag your finger up the touchscreen. Touch the data plan (or 'package') you require and click Next.

Figure 2.13

5. Enter your payment information and address.

6. Read and agree to the terms and conditions. You can scroll the terms and conditions by touching and dragging them.

7. You will see a message confirming that the data plan (or package) has been activated.

8. To see how much of your data allowance is still available, go into Settings, Mobile Data, then tap View Account. Note that your remaining data might be shown in MB, and that 1GB is equal to 1024MB.

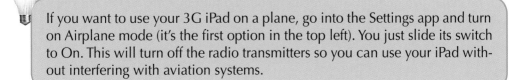

If you want to use your 3G iPad on a plane, go into the Settings app and turn on Airplane mode (it's the first option in the top left). You just slide its switch to On. This will turn off the radio transmitters so you can use your iPad without interfering with aviation systems.

Understanding your Internet connection

In the status bar, in the top left corner of your iPad, you can see some icons representing the status of your Internet connection. Most of the time when you're using the Internet, you'll see a fan symbol, which shows that Wi-Fi is working (see Figure 2.14). The more lines there are on the fan, the stronger the Wi-Fi signal is.

If you have a 3G iPad, you will also see a bar graph indicating the strength of the mobile communications network and the name of your mobile operator. Your iPad will use Wi-Fi whenever it's available and will automatically switch to the mobile network when it's not.

Your iPad will use the best quality mobile network connection available, and you will see a 3G, E or round circle icon in the status bar, depending on what type of connection your iPad is using. The 3G connection is fastest, and the GPRS network, represented by the round circle, is slowest.

When you see those symbols, you're using up your allocation in your data plan, so don't go crazy downloading movies. To stop the mobile communications network from being used, go into the settings, tap Mobile Data and then switch it off.

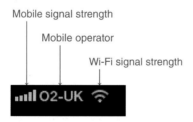

Mobile signal strength

Mobile operator

Wi-Fi signal strength

Figure 2.14

If you're in a geographic area that your 3G provider doesn't cover, the data roaming feature might still enable you to get a connection through another provider. It can be expensive, though, so I recommend you turn that off. You'll find it in the Settings app, under Mobile Data.

Remember that if you're using 3G and have a limited data allowance, any web pages, maps, apps, music or videos you download will eat into that data allowance. It's cheaper, and faster, to use Wi-Fi where available.

Securing your iPad

There are a number of settings you can use to protect your iPad from loss or unauthorised use. Even if you don't have any valuable data on your iPad, these settings can help to protect younger family members from content they shouldn't see online, and to protect your wallet from the risk of them accidentally buying hundreds of apps on your account!

Adjusting the parental controls (restrictions)

To restrict the content that can be viewed on your iPad, go into the Settings, tap General and then tap Restrictions. Tap Enable Restrictions at the top of the screen and you will be prompted to enter a four digit passcode, twice, just to make sure that it's entered correctly.

You can then restrict access to the web (Safari), Internet videos (YouTube) and Apple's music store (iTunes), and can stop users installing or deleting apps. You can also decide whether to allow the location to be changed in Maps, and whether email accounts may be changed. In-App Purchases enable people to buy content while they're using an app, and you can restrict explicit music, films with certain certificates, and TV shows and apps unsuitable for younger audiences. There are also settings to stop users playing multiplayer games and adding friends in Game Center.

To disable restrictions again, you'll need your passcode, so don't forget it!

Setting a passcode for your iPad

You can protect your iPad from unauthorised access by requiring a passcode to be entered before it can be unlocked. To do this, go into your General settings again, and tap Turn Passcode On. As with the passcode for restrictions, the iPad will ask you to enter it twice to make sure you don't mistype it.

If you turn off the Simple Passcode, you can have a longer password using a combination of letters and numbers.

You can also set the switch so that all the iPad's content is erased after someone enters the passcode incorrectly 10 times. This helps to protect your data if your iPad is lost or stolen, but isn't recommended for anyone who's ever forgotten a password and has had to keep trying different possibilities!

When you connect your iPad to your computer, its content is backed up on your computer. If you are ever unlucky enough to lose your iPad, you can copy the backup of your iPad from your computer to a new iPad when you set it up or restore it (see later in this chapter).

Setting up Find my iPad

Apple's free Find my iPad service helps you to recover your iPad if it is ever lost or stolen. It enables you to log into a web browser to see where your iPad is on a map, enables you to send a message on the iPad screen to whoever has found it, and even enables you to set a passcode remotely or delete all its contents to stop someone else getting your sensitive data.

To set up Find my iPad, follow these steps:

1. Go into your iPad Settings. Tap Mail, Contacts, Calendars and then tap Add Account.

2. Tap MobileMe and log in using your Apple ID. This is the same as the iTunes store ID you created when setting up your iPad. Accept the terms and conditions.

3. Check your email for a message from Apple. You need to click the link in it, and then sign in using your Apple ID to confirm your email address works. You can use your computer to do this step if you don't have email set up on your iPad.

4. On your iPad, return to the Mail, Contacts and Calendars settings. Click MobileMe and, when prompted, allow MobileMe to use the location of your iPad. Ensure Find my iPad is switched on.

5. Tap Done in the top right of the MobileMe Settings to finish.

6. To test it's working, visit **www.me.com** in a web browser on your computer and log in. The map will show you where your iPad is, and you can click the arrow beside your iPad's name to send a message or lock it. If you lose it on your own desk (it can happen!), you can even get it to issue a sonar-like distress signal, so you can track it down. This works even if the iPad's volume is switched off.

Making your iPad easier to use

For those who have impaired vision or hearing, there are several settings that make the iPad easier to use. You can find them by going into the Settings app, tapping General on the left and then tapping Accessibility:

● **VoiceOver:** This reads the iPad screen aloud for the benefit of people who cannot see the screen. It also enables a comprehensive set of gestures for navigating content and entering information. When using the keyboard, for example, you can flick left or right to advance through the keys and have them read aloud. A double-tap enters the character chosen. VoiceOver completely changes the way the iPad is used. I won't be covering it further in this book but if you believe you might benefit from it, the iPad manual provides comprehensive guidance.

● **Zoom:** If you have impaired vision, you can use the Zoom feature to magnify the iPad screen. Once it is switched on, you zoom in by tapping the screen twice in quick succession, using three fingers both times. To change which bit of the screen you are looking at, touch the screen with three fingers and move them in any direction on the glass surface. To increase or decrease the magnification, tap with three fingers and then quickly tap again with those fingers and keep them on the glass. Move your fingers up the glass to zoom in, and down to zoom out. It sounds complicated, but you can practise on the screen for Zoom settings. You can use any combination of fingers and thumbs from any hands. You don't have to use three fingers next to each other if that feels awkward. This feature is really only for those with impaired vision who need to enlarge everything on the iPad's screen, including its buttons. In Chapter 7, you'll learn the pinch gesture, which is an easy way for everyone to magnify web pages and photos.

● **Large Text:** This increases the size of the text in emails and notes. It can be used in combination with the Zoom features to help you see the other elements of those apps.

● **White on Black:** This reverses the colour scheme so the text is white on a black background. There is a side effect: icons and images also have their colours reversed, so they look like negatives.

● **Mono Audio:** Stereo audio works by delivering different parts of the sound to different ears. Those with poor hearing in one ear might miss part of the sound, so the mono audio setting enables you to hear the complete soundtrack in each ear.

● **Speak Auto-text:** If you turn this on, the iPad will speak its text corrections as you type. This is a useful feature for everyone, and works independently of VoiceOver. You'll learn more about this in Chapter 3.

● **Triple-click Home:** This provides a quick shortcut to manage Voice Over or White on Black. When activated, you can press the Home button three times in quick succession to turn them on or off.

Adjusting other iPad settings

The iPad is a sophisticated machine and has many settings you can adjust. Thankfully, you can ignore the vast majority of them, but here are a few you might want to know about:

● **Brightness:** To change the screen brightness, go into Settings and tap Brightness and Wallpaper. Touch the round button and slide it right or left to increase or decrease brightness. The Auto-Brightness setting adjusts the brightness automatically, depending on how much light there is in the room.

● **Wallpaper:** The wallpaper is the image in the background of your iPad's locked and Home screens. To change it, go into your Brightness & Wallpaper settings and then click the iPad picture. You can choose from 30 images provided by Apple, or from any of your own photos on the iPad.

● **Sounds:** To stop getting a sound alert when you type on the keyboard, or when you lock or unlock the device or get email, go into your General Settings and then choose Sounds.

- **Volume:** The easiest way to change the volume is to hold the iPad with the Home button at the bottom, and find the 'rocker' switch towards the top of the right edge. This clicks in two directions to turn the sound up or down. There is also a slider switch near the volume control that mutes the device. When the volume is down, you can still hear keyboard clicks, ringtones and other sounds enabled in your settings. When the device is muted using the slider, you hear nothing. When you use these buttons, the iPad screen shows you the volume change or mute status in the middle of the screen.

- **Reset:** To reset some or all of your settings, go into your General settings and then click Reset. This gives you several options. If you choose 'Reset all settings', the iPad's settings will be set to their factory defaults, but your information on the device (including your contacts and music) will be unaffected. If you choose 'Erase all content and settings', your data will be deleted from the iPad and all the iPad's settings will be set to their factory defaults. You can also reset the network settings (including for Wi-Fi networks), reset the dictionary (used for Auto-text, which you'll learn about in Chapter 3), reset the Home screen layout (see Chapter 12) and reset location warnings (which are normally presented once for each app that tries to use your location; if you reset the warnings you'll be asked again for each app).

You can configure the mute switch so that it locks the iPad orientation instead of muting your iPad. That means when you turn the device, the screen contents don't rotate as they usually do. It can be a handy feature if you're reading or watching TV at an angle in bed. Go into the Settings app, tap General, and then change the option for 'Use Side Switch' to 'Lock Rotation'. You can change it back again at any time.

Troubleshooting and fixing your iPad

If you experience problems with your iPad, there are two things you can do. Firstly, you can check whether there is a software update available for the iPad. It's worth doing this from time to time anyway, because Apple often introduces new iPad features in its software. You can update the software on your iPad without affecting any of the information, apps, music or other files stored on it, and the update is a free service. To update your iPad, connect it to your computer, go into the iTunes software on it, and click 'Check for Update' in the Summary pane (see Figure 2.5). When iTunes knows an update is available, this button is instead labelled 'Update'.

You can also update the iTunes software running on your computer. Apple regularly introduces new features and fixes bugs that come to light. In the iTunes software, click Help at the top, and then click 'Check for Updates'.

If your iPad still appears to be faulty and you can't find a solution online, you can also 'restore' your iPad, as a last resort. This deletes everything from your iPad and reverts its settings to those of a new iPad so you have to start setting it up from scratch. Whenever you connect your iPad to your computer, your iPad is backed up, though, so when you restore, you'll be given the option to copy the last available backup from your computer to your restored iPad. If you can, you should synchronise your iPad with your computer to update the backup copy on your computer before you restore your iPad. If you have a recent enough backup, you should be able to restore your iPad without losing information or apps from it, but you'll still have to go through the basic stages of setting up the iPad. To restore your iPad, connect it to your computer and in the iTunes software click 'Restore' in the Summary pane (see Figure 2.5).

Now that you've been using the iPad for a while, it will be covered in finger marks. Give it a gentle rub with a cloth for cleaning spectacles. The finger marks look worse when the device is off: when it's on, the screen shines through them no problem. For stubborn marks, Apple suggests a "soft, slightly damp, lint-free cloth" but advises you to take care not to get moisture in the iPad's openings. Never use cleaning agents or abrasives.

Summary

- iTunes is free software for your computer that is used to manage the content on your iPad.

- Before you can use your iPad, you need to install the iTunes software on your computer and connect your iPad to your computer.

- The best way to charge your iPad is to connect it to the mains.

- To turn on your iPad, press and hold the Sleep/Wake button.

- Use the skin of your fingers on the touchscreen, not your fingernails.

- You can use the iPad any way up, and the screen display will rotate so that it's always the right way up for you.

- iPad activities take place within software applications, called 'apps'.

- You can find icons for your apps on your Home screen.

- Touch an app icon to start the app.

- The Settings app is used to set up your Wi-Fi connection, 3G connection, passcodes and features to improve ease of use.

- To slide a switch on the screen, touch it and move your finger across the iPad screen or simply tap it.

- The iPad has a keyboard that appears on screen when you need to type something in, such as a password. To hide it again, tap the button in the bottom right of it.

- When you type a password on the iPad, each character appears briefly on the screen, so take care that nobody's looking over your shoulder.

- You can change the image in the background of your Home screen by changing your wallpaper settings.

- Don't use cleaning agents or abrasives on your iPad. Use a cloth for cleaning spectacles to rub away any smudges.

Brain training

Now your iPad is set up, you're ready to begin using it. You can refer back to this chapter if you need to change your settings in future, but for now, let's have a quick quiz to refresh your memory. There might be more than one right answer.

1. You can charge your iPad by:

(a) Connecting it to a power socket

(b) Connecting it to a computer, with the computer in sleep mode and the iPad switched on

(c) Connecting it to a computer, with the computer switched on and the iPad in sleep mode

(d) Connecting it to your computer keyboard

2. You can use your iPad:

(a) In a landscape orientation

(b) In a portrait orientation

(c) With the Home button at the top

(d) Back to front

3. When you see a E in the top left of your iPad, it means:

(a) An entertainment app is running

(b) You're connected to the mobile network on a 3G iPad

(c) You're connected to Wi-Fi

(d) That's today's letter on Sesame Street

4. To protect the data on your iPad, you can:

(a) Delete its contents remotely if it gets stolen

(b) Make it delete your data if someone enters the password wrongly 10 times

(c) Add a password to stop someone else unlocking it

(d) Stop others from deleting apps without a password

5. To silence the locking sound on your iPad:

(a) Push the Sleep/Wake button really gently

(b) Slide the slider on the side of your iPad

(c) Adjust your sound settings

(d) Put your iPad in a case

Answers

Q1 – a and c   **Q2** – a, b or c   **Q3** – b   **Q4** – a, b, c and d   **Q5** – b and c

Keeping notes on your iPad

3

Equipment needed: An iPad that is ready to use, and reasonably clean fingers!

Skills needed: Knowledge of how to start apps (see Chapter 2).

Now that you have your iPad set up and have learned how to navigate its apps, it's time to start using it. In this chapter, you'll learn how to use the Notes app, which is one of the simplest apps that comes with your iPad, inspired by a humble pad of paper. Whether you're writing a shopping list, a song or a story, Notes is there in an instant to capture your ideas before they drift away. When you need to refer back to a note, the search function makes it easy to find.

Although you can email your notes to people, the Notes app is not intended for creating polished final documents for sharing. There are no features for bold text, underlining, different fonts or any other changes in formatting that you might be used to from a word processing package. At first, that might sound like a limitation, but it's actually a strength: there is nothing distracting or unnecessary on the screen, so you can focus on what you're writing. If you're one of those people who has to fiddle with 15 fonts before you start writing, you're all out of excuses. You don't even have to save your work. Notes takes care of that for you automatically.

You've already seen the keyboard when you were entering passwords to set up your internet connection. In this chapter, you'll have an opportunity to practise using it and will also see how the iPad's predictive text feature (called Auto-text) can help you to write more quickly.

To start the Notes app, tap the Notes icon on the Home screen.

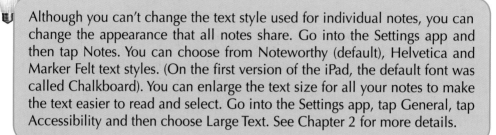

Although you can't change the text style used for individual notes, you can change the appearance that all notes share. Go into the Settings app and then tap Notes. You can choose from Noteworthy (default), Helvetica and Marker Felt text styles. (On the first version of the iPad, the default font was called Chalkboard). You can enlarge the text size for all your notes to make the text easier to read and select. Go into the Settings app, tap General, tap Accessibility and then choose Large Text. See Chapter 2 for more details.

Understanding the Notes screen

Notes is a good example of an app that adapts to make best use of the screen space depending on which way up your iPad is. Figure 3.1 shows Notes in portrait mode, where the screen is filled with blank paper. To see a list of your notes, or to search them, you need to tap the Notes button in the top left, as I have in Figure 3.1.

Figure 3.2 shows what Notes looks like in landscape mode. You can see less of each note at a time, but there is a permanent panel on the left that lists your notes and enables you to search them. I prefer the landscape mode because it gives me a bigger keyboard too, so I can type more quickly.

You can use whichever orientation suits you best. When you're using other apps in future, it's worth rotating the screen to see if it declutters the screen or makes additional features easier to find and use.

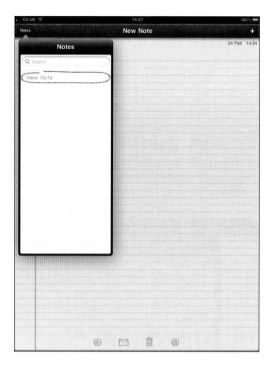

Figure 3.1

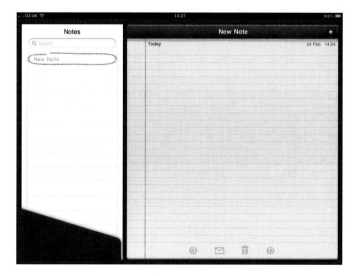

Figure 3.2

Writing your first note

When Notes opens for the first time, it shows what looks like a blank piece of yellow paper. Tap this, and the keyboard will appear so that you can start typing.

Choose your first words carefully: there are no filenames in Notes because your work is saved automatically without any intervention from you. Instead, the first few words you write in a note will be used to refer to it in the list of notes. If you start your note with a short title, such as 'Lasagne Recipe', your notes will be easier to navigate. If your first line reads 'My note about the way to make lasagne', all you'll see in the list of notes will be an unhelpful 'My note about the…' (see Figure 3.3).

Figure 3.3

Using the iPad keyboard

Some of the keys on the iPad keyboard are set out in the same way as a normal keyboard. The space bar runs along the bottom in the middle, and the standard QWERTYUIOP layout for letters is present and correct.

In the top right, you can see the Delete key (see Figure 3.3). Tap this to remove a character, or keep your finger on the key to keep deleting, first a character at a time and then a word at a time.

There are two Shift keys, but they work a bit differently to a normal keyboard. You can hold down the Shift key while you tap a letter key to type a capital letter as you would on a normal keyboard, but it might feel a bit awkward. Instead, you can tap a Shift key and then tap a letter. When the Shift key has been activated, the arrow in it turns blue. After you tap a letter, the Shift key is deactivated again.

To speed up your typing, the iPad helps you to start a new sentence with a capital letter. When you finish a sentence with a full stop and a space, the keyboard automatically turns the Shift key on for the next letter. If you forget about this and tap the Shift key, you'll turn it off again so your sentence will start with a lower case letter instead. When the Shift key has automatically been activated for you, the arrow in it is outlined in blue (as you can see in Figure 3.3).

There's no separate Caps Lock key, but if you tap a Shift key twice in quick succession, caps lock is switched on. If the whole of the Shift key except the arrow is blue, it means that caps lock is on and any letters typed will be capitalised until you tap Shift again.

If you tap something twice quickly, it's called a double-tap, a bit like an iPad version of the double-click you might use on a mouse. If the gap between your taps is too long, the iPad might think you made two separate single taps instead, so keep it snappy!

As with a normal keyboard, you can use the Shift key to get different symbols from some other keys. Using Shift with the comma key enters an exclamation mark, for example.

When you reach the end of a line, keep typing and you will automatically be moved to the start of the next line. To start a new line at any time, press the Return key. You can press it twice to leave a blank line, to make it easier to see the gaps between paragraphs. When you start a new line, the Shift key is activated so that the first letter will be capitalised. If you don't want that, tap the Shift key to turn it off before you type your first letter.

Don't worry about running out of space on the screen: a note is like a never-ending sheet of paper. You can write as much or as little on it as you want, although you might find it easier to use lots of short notes rather than a few long ones. If your note is too long for it all to fit on the screen at the same time, you can scroll it up or down by touching the note and dragging your finger up or down the screen. The iPad is smart enough to know that if you drag your finger, you didn't intend to tap or select anything on the screen.

You can tap the space bar twice quickly at the end of a sentence to enter a full stop and a space.

Entering special characters

Using the simple keyboard, you should be able to type shopping lists and simple notes. But what happens when you want to jot down a recipe with all the quantities of ingredients, or need to complete your Spanish homework with all its accents? For situations like this, you need to learn about the more advanced features of the iPad keyboard.

The iPad makes it easier to enter accents than it has been on any other computer keyboard I've owned. If you want to enter an accented character, just tap the letter key and hold your finger on it. A bubble appears above the key, showing the letter with different accents applied (see the E key in Figure 3.3). Without removing your finger from the touchscreen, slide it to the version of the letter you want. When you release your finger, the letter with the accent will be added to your note.

Even if you don't use any foreign languages, this is a useful technique to learn. You can use it on the full stop key to type speech marks, and can use it on the comma key to enter an apostrophe or single quote mark. As you'll see in Chapter 7, it can also help you to enter website addresses more quickly.

There are also two special keyboards you can use to enter numbers and symbols. Press the '.?123' key and all the keys will change to the keyboard shown in Figure 3.4. This keyboard shows the numbers and most often used punctuation symbols. It also has an Undo key you can use if you make a mistake in deleting or typing text.

Do you remember the Etch-a-Sketch toy that was about the same size as an iPad and enabled you to draw pictures using two dials and delete them again by shaking it? Perhaps as a tribute to that classic toy, you can also undo by shaking the iPad, although it's easier to tap the Undo key.

Figure 3.4

As with the letters keyboard, some of these keys have additional symbols that you can find by pressing and holding a key. The £ key, for example, provides quick access to other currency symbols. The apostrophe and speech mark keys provide several different styles (including proper 66 and 99 shaped quote marks). To enter a bullet point, press and hold the dash key until that symbol appears. The full stop key can also be used to enter an ellipsis (three dots in a row).

There is a third keyboard that offers a range of less frequently used symbols (see Figure 3.5), such as square and curly brackets, the percent sign, and currency symbols. It also has a Redo key to allow you to reinstate something you undo without meaning to. To show this keyboard, press the '#+=' key that replaces the Shift key on the numbers keyboard (Figure 3.4).

To go back to the letter keyboard from either of the other keyboards, tap the ABC key. To help you type fluently, the iPad automatically switches to the letter keyboard after you type a space or apostrophe.

Hide keyboard

Figure 3.5

Hiding the keyboard

The only problem with the keyboard is that it gets in the way of the note itself, which can make it hard to re-read your note. At any time, you can hide the keyboard by tapping the Hide Keyboard key at the bottom right of the keyboard, indicated in Figure 3.5. It's on every version of the keyboard, and you can bring the keyboard back again simply by tapping the note to start typing.

Although it takes a little time to adjust to the feel of the onscreen keyboard, it is possible to type quickly, and Notes provides the ideal place to practise your typing. Give it a go!

Using Auto-text to speed up your writing

You already know about some of the amazing things the iPad can do, but did you know it can predict the future? Okay, so maybe that's stretching it a bit. But it gives it a good go. Try writing the word 'onomatopoeia'. You only need to tap four characters before the iPad guesses what you're intending to type, and shows it in a small bubble underneath your typing (see Figure 3.6).

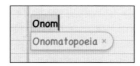

Figure 3.6

What you're seeing is the Auto-text feature, and you might already have noticed it working while you were entering text before. It's like a cross between the predictive text feature of a mobile phone, and the automatic spelling correction feature of a word processor. It aims to enable you to type more quickly and accurately, but if you're not careful, the iPad can change words you don't want it to.

The word 'book' became slang for 'good' thanks to the predictive text feature of mobile phones, because when you try to enter 'cool' in a text message it often comes out as 'book'.

To accept the iPad's suggestion, just tap the space bar. It doesn't matter how far into the word you are. If the iPad can guess it in four characters, you don't have to type any more and you're spared the trouble of remembering that horrible pile-up of vowels that comes at the end of our example word.

If the iPad makes an incorrect suggestion, keep typing your word and it will keep trying to guess. Whenever it gets it right, tap the space bar.

The problem comes if you get to the end of the word, and the iPad thinks you're midway through typing something else or thinks you've misspelled something you haven't. Try typing the word 'ill', for example. When you tap the space bar, the iPad will replace your correct and complete word with 'I'll', which is used more often but which makes no sense in your sentence. To stop this happening, touch the iPad's suggested word on the screen and it will go away. This feels a bit counterintuitive, because usually you touch things to select them, but touching an Auto-text suggestion dismisses it. That's why there's a cross to the right of the Auto-text suggestion: when you touch it, you close it.

If Auto-text makes a change you don't want, use the Delete key to go back to the end of the word, and a new bubble will appear above the word showing what you originally typed. Touch this, and your text will replace the Auto-text. The iPad is programmed to learn from you over time so it can improve its suggestions to you.

In the accessibility settings of your iPad (see Chapter 2), you can set the iPad to speak Auto-text suggestions out loud, even if you don't use VoiceOver. This can be a good way to make sure you notice the suggestions when you're typing quickly or looking at the keyboard. If you can't hear the suggestions, check your iPad's volume is turned up.

Editing your text

Sometimes, you'll want to change what you've written in a note. You might spot a mistake you made when you first typed it, or might need to update it with new information or remove items you've bought from a shopping list. The editing features of the iPad have some similarities with other computers, but also introduce some new ideas.

Positioning the insertion point

The insertion point is what Apple calls the cursor, the vertical flashing line that indicates where characters will be added when you type. As with a word processor, when you press the Delete key, characters to the left of the insertion point are removed.

To reposition the insertion point, just tap your note in the place you would like the insertion point to appear, and it will jump to the end of the nearest word.

You can't put the insertion point in the middle of an empty space on the page. If you tap in the space after the last piece of text in your note, the insertion point will go to the end of your text. To create blank space between bits of text, add some blank lines with the Return key.

If you want to move to the middle of a word, tap the word and hold your finger on the screen. You might find it easier to do this accurately if you make the text larger, using the Accessibility options in the Settings app (see Chapter 2).

A magnifying glass appears above the insertion point (see Figure 3.7) to show you where the insertion point is in your word, which gets around the problem of your finger obscuring your view. As you move your finger left or right, the insertion point will move through the word, and you will be able to see it in the magnifying glass. When you remove your finger, the insertion point stays where you moved it using the magnifying glass.

> For instance: I name the most famous racehorses of all time, Red Rum and Shergar. e what I mble beasts, famous decades after they died. What do then a Taurus mon? I'll tell you: two vowels in their names. Can yo the to failed racehorses with two vowels in their names? No. See mean! And did you know that a Pisces jockey never wins with a Taurus horse, too? Hundreds of tiny details like these come together to decide the outcome of the race.

Figure 3.7

Once you have positioned your insertion point, you can add or delete characters using the keyboard.

Using cut, copy and paste

Sometimes, you might want to move a chunk of text around, and perhaps even move it from one application to another. You might want to copy something from a web page into a note, for example, or put part of a note into an email you're writing. The Notes app enables you to select chunks of text so that you can move them around within Notes or between different applications.

The first step is to select the piece of text you want to use. There are three ways to do this in the Notes app:

- Tap the insertion point. A menu will appear, with the options Select and Select All. Tap Select, and the nearest word will be selected. Tap Select All, and all the content of the note will be selected.

- Tap and hold your finger on a word anywhere in your note. The magnifying glass appears so you can position your insertion point. When you lift your finger, the menu appears with the options to Select or Select All.

- Double-tap a word to select it.

You can tell what text has been selected because it's highlighted in blue. There's also a menu above it, which we'll come to in a moment. First, take a look at the vertical lines at the start and end of the selected text (see Figure 3.8). Each has a bobble on the end, called a grab point. To increase or decrease the area selected, you touch a grab point and move your finger across the screen. A rectangular magnifier helps you to see what you're selecting. This is how you select a few words, sentences or paragraphs, or even just a few characters.

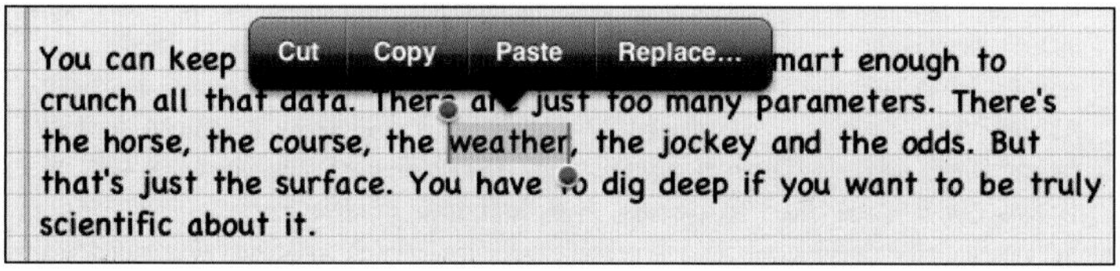

You can keep [Cut] [Copy] [Paste] [Replace...] mart enough to crunch all that data. There are just too many parameters. There's the horse, the course, the weather, the jockey and the odds. But that's just the surface. You have to dig deep if you want to be truly scientific about it.

Figure 3.8

Spend a few minutes practising selecting text, including sentences and paragraphs. It doesn't take long to get the hang of it, but it is one of the more fiddly techniques to learn on the iPad.

The menu above your selected text will show you some or all of the following options (Figure 3.8):

- **Cut:** If you cut a piece of text, it will be removed from your note but will be temporarily kept in the iPad's memory. You can then insert your text in a different place in your note, by pasting it there.

- **Copy:** If you copy a piece of text, it will be left where it is now, but a temporary copy of it will be made so that you can paste it (insert it) somewhere else in your note as well.

- **Paste:** If you select some text on screen and then choose Paste, it will delete the text you have selected and paste the last piece of text you cut or copied in its place. You won't need to use this option often.

- **Replace:** If you select a word and choose Replace, the spellchecker will suggest alternative words to replace the one you've selected. When you tap one of the suggestions, it will replace the original word with your new selected word.

To select one of the menu options (Cut, Copy, Paste or Replace), you just tap it. To change your mind and do nothing, tap the selected text or tap somewhere else in the note.

When you're moving text around in your note, most of the time you just need to select the text, copy or cut it, move the insertion point where you want to paste it back in, and then tap the insertion point. If some text has been cut or copied, there will be a Paste option you can tap to insert it in your note.

The iPad can only 'remember' one chunk of text at a time, so be careful not to lose anything – take particular care when cutting text. When you cut a piece of text it is removed from your note but kept in the iPad's memory. If you then cut or copy another piece of text before pasting the first one, the iPad forgets your first piece of text and you can't get it back.

If you want to delete a chunk of text, select it in the same way and then tap the Delete key on the keyboard. If you've hidden the keyboard, tap the note to show it again before you select your text.

Fixing your spelling

The iPad will give you a helping hand and fix some of your spelling as you type. You might even find yourself depending on some of its suggestions to speed up your typing. There's no need to tap Shift before the letter 'I' if you're talking about yourself, because the iPad will change the word 'i' to 'I'; and if you type 'ive' it will automatically change it to 'I've'.

The iPad is less confident about correcting other spellings, but if a word isn't in the dictionary it will underline it with red dots (see 'peopl' in the first line in Figure 3.9). When you tap the word, suggestions for the correct spelling will appear from the dictionary (see 'wil' in the last line in Figure 3.9). You can tap one of these suggestions to replace your original word with it.

Of course, if the correct word isn't in the dictionary, you can edit it yourself in the normal way by repositioning the insertion point and using the keyboard to add or delete characters.

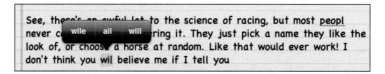

Figure 3.9

Adding and deleting notes

When you started Notes for the first time, it opened with a blank note, ready to receive your wisdom. When you want to write additional notes, you need to tap the Add Note button (the one with the plus sign at the top right, see Figure 3.10). That will open a new blank page, but your previous note will remain in the app for you to refer back to at any time.

You can also delete notes by going to a note and then tapping the bin icon at the bottom of it (Figure 3.10). A red box will appear saying 'Delete Note'. Tap that to get rid of your note, or tap somewhere else to keep your note.

You can browse through your notes using the Previous Note and Next Note icons.

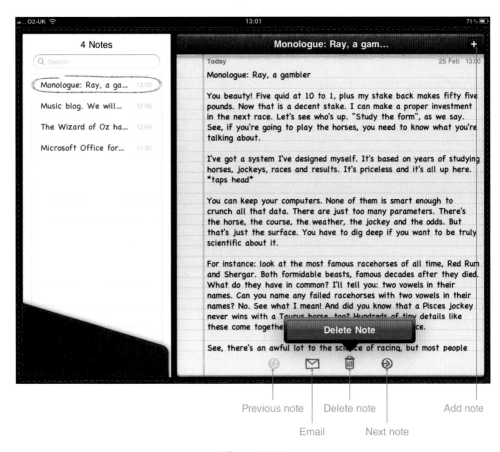

Figure 3.10

 There is no undo for deleting notes, so don't delete something you might regret!

Emailing notes

At the bottom of each note is an icon that looks like an envelope (see Figure 3.10), which you can tap to email a note to someone. Chapter 5 shows you how to set up email on your iPad, so that you can use this button to quickly share what you've written.

Searching your notes

I have a stack of wire-bound notebooks and often spend time thumbing through them trying to find something I jotted down weeks or even months ago. The iPad saves you that kind of hassle because it has a search capability built into it. Depending on what you use Notes for, this can be a powerful tool. If you keep recipes in Notes, for example, you could search by ingredient to see what you can concoct from what's left in the fridge. If you're using Notes to keep track of DIY jobs, you could search by room or by tool to help you plan your weekend.

When you're writing notes, think about the kind of words you might want to use to find them later. You might even want to add a few words to the end of a note that you might want to search by, just to make it easy to find the note later.

Using the search in Notes

The search panel in Notes is shown on the left of the screen in landscape mode, or pops up when you press the Notes button in portrait mode. It lists your most recently updated notes, with the latest at the top of the list, and a snippet showing the first few words to help you to tell them apart. The current note is circled in crayon (see Figure 3.10) and you can choose any of the others by tapping it in the list.

To search your notes, tap the search box at the top of the search panel (see Figure 3.11). You then use the keyboard to enter a word or phrase from the note. It doesn't have to be from the beginning, or even be a complete word. Anything that you can remember from the note can be used to find it again.

As you type, the iPad will search through your notes and narrow the list of notes underneath the search box to those that feature the word or phrase you're looking for. When you've found the note you need, tap it in the list and you'll be taken to it.

While you're typing in the search box, a cross in a circle appears in the right of the search box (see Figure 3.11). Tap this to cancel what you've entered. You'll see this used in lots of other apps in future.

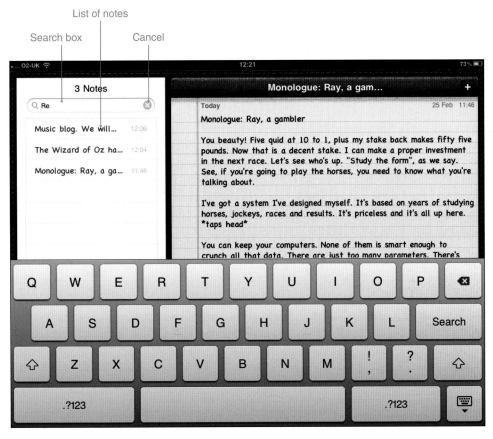

Figure 3.11

Using the iPad's Spotlight search

There's another way to search Notes and other content on your iPad. The Spotlight search rummages through all the built-in apps to find a note, photo, email or other file that you're looking for. It can also find apps by name, and provides a shortcut for searching the Internet, or for searching the online encyclopaedia Wikipedia.

Wikipedia is an encyclopaedia that anyone can help to write. It has more than 3.5 million articles in English, and 91,000 active contributors. Its coverage of popular culture is much stronger than conventional encyclopaedias, but it has been criticised in the past for some high-profile inaccuracies.

To go to the Spotlight search, press the Home button to return to the Home screen and place your finger somewhere in the middle of it. Move your finger quickly to the right, and lift it. This gesture is called a flick. The Spotlight search screen will roll into view from the left. To go back again, you can put your finger in the middle of the search screen (above the keyboard) and flick it to the left. It doesn't matter if you touch an icon when you flick. As long as your finger moves, the iPad will work out that you intended to flick the screen, not tap the icon.

The Spotlight search looks like Figure 3.12. Once you've added songs, films, contacts and more to your iPad, Spotlight will help you to find them all. Until then, it can help you to find notes and apps on the device.

When the Spotlight search appears, type what you are searching for into the search bar at the top of the screen. As with the search in the Notes app, the search results update as you type. Your notes will appear in the search results with an excerpt from the start of the note. Tap a note extract to go straight to that note. If you can't find what you're looking for, tap the Cancel button in the right-hand corner of the search box to start again.

When you come to install your own apps later, Spotlight can save you a lot of time hunting around to find the icons. If you want to try starting apps using Spotlight, try searching for 'calendar' 'notes', and 'maps'.

Try moving between the Home screen and the Spotlight search screen using the flick gesture, to practise the technique. The flick gesture is used in many apps, including Notes, to rapidly scroll through content. If you have a long note, try flicking up on it to scroll through it quickly.

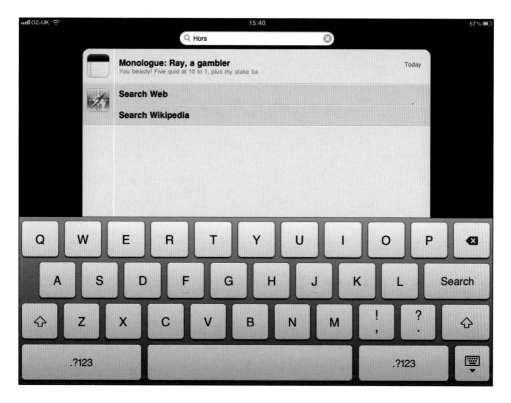

Figure 3.12

As you install your own apps, additional Home screens will be added and you use the flick to move between them too. From the Home screen, flicking right takes you to the search and flicking left takes you to the next Home screen full of apps. If you try flicking left from the Home screen now, you'll see the icons move a little and then bounce back because there isn't another screen of apps to go to.

You can also use the Home button to move between the search screen and the Home screen. If you press the Home button when you're on the Home screen, it will take you to the Spotlight search. If you press the Home button from the search screen, you go back to the Home screen. But where's the fun in that? Buttons are so last century — it's all about gestures now!

Summary

- Notes is an app that is used for writing, reading and searching text, from shopping lists to stories.

- You can't change the formatting of individual notes, but you can change the appearance of all notes to make the app easier to use.

- You can use Notes in portrait or landscape orientation. The keyboard is bigger if you choose landscape.

- Touch a note to make the keyboard appear.

- You can tap the Shift key and then press a letter to enter a capital letter. Double-tap Shift to switch the caps lock on.

- There are two special keyboards for numbers and symbols.

- If you press and hold on some keys, additional options will appear, such as accented letters.

- You can undo by tapping the Undo button on the numbers keyboard or by shaking the iPad, which is more therapeutic.

- Auto-text tries to predict what you're typing. To accept a suggestion, tap the space bar. To reject it, tap the suggested word on the screen or just type the rest of your word.

- Tap your note to position the insertion point. To position it more precisely, tap and hold until the magnifying glass appears, and then move your finger left or right.

- There are several ways to select your text. Use the grab points to increase or decrease the area selected.

- You can cut, copy and paste text.

- To see suggested spelling corrections, tap a word that's underlined with red dots.

- You can search your notes within the Notes app, or you can use the Spotlight search, which searches all the content on the built-in apps on your iPad.

Brain training

Congratulations — you've mastered your first iPad app! Before we move on to explore how you can use the iPad for communications, take a moment to try this quick quiz.

1. To make it easy to find notes again later, it's a good idea to:

(a) Put a simple title in the first few words of the note

(b) Add a few words to the end of the note, which you might want to search for later

(c) Use as many obscure words as possible

(d) Check your spelling's right, to make sure that any words you search for can be found in the note

2. To enter quote marks in your note, you can:

(a) Go to the numbers keyboard

(b) Go to the special symbols keyboard

(c) Press and hold the full stop key on the letter keyboard

(d) Press the space bar twice

3. If Auto-text correctly guesses a word you're typing, you should:

(a) Tap the suggestion to accept it

(b) Press the space bar

(c) Keep typing your word

(d) Press Delete

4. To position the insertion point in the middle of a word:

(a) Tap the word

(b) Double-tap the word

(c) Tap and hold the word, and then move the insertion point when the magnifying glass appears

(d) Tap the middle of your note

5. To go to the Spotlight search, you can:

(a) Go to the Home screen and press the Home button

(b) Tap the search box in the top left of the Notes app

(c) Go to the Home screen and flick right

(d) Go to the Home screen and flick left

Answers

Q1 – a, b, and d   **Q2** – a, b, or c   **Q3** – b   **Q4** – c   **Q5** – a and c

PART II
Using Your iPad for Communications

I've just emailed all our friends, to tell them what losers they are for using clunky, old-fashioned laptops and desktops.

Managing your address book and birthday list

4

Equipment needed: Your iPad and your address book (whether it's on your computer or scrawled in a beaten up old paper notebook).

Skills needed: Experience starting apps (see Chapter 3), entering information into the iPad (see Chapter 2) and using the iPad keyboard (see Chapter 3).

One of the most useful pieces of information you can carry with you is your address book. If you remember a birthday at the last minute and have to write out a card in the shop, or just want to phone a friend for advice or a chat, you'll be pleased to have your addresses and phone numbers at the tip of your fingers.

The iPad comes with an app called Contacts, which is designed to help you manage your address book. It's a simple app but it's powerful because it's integrated with many other apps. When you're sending email, you can use the details in your address book to save you having to remember or type in somebody's email address, for example, and the Maps app enables you to find directions to and from your friends' houses quickly.

In this chapter, I'll show you how to manage your contacts on your iPad, including synchronising them with other contacts software on your computer and adding new contacts using your iPad. I'll also show you how the Calendar app can be used to view your friends' birthdays month by month.

Synchronising contacts from your computer

If you already manage your contacts on your computer, you might be able to copy them to your iPad automatically and keep them synchronised in future, so that when you make changes or additions on your iPad, your computer will be updated when you connect them up again, and vice versa.

You're in luck if you have contacts stored in Microsoft Outlook (2003 or later), Microsoft Outlook Express, Windows Contacts or Windows Address Book , or you are using Mac OS X Address Book on the Mac. Both Windows Mail and Windows Live Mail store information using Windows Contacts, so if you have stored contact details using those applications, you will be able to copy them to your iPad too. You can also synchronise with Yahoo Address Book and Google Contacts, if you use those.

If you don't keep any contacts on your computer, you can skip this step and go straight to 'Browsing your contacts'. If you set your contacts to synchronise with Windows Contacts or a Mac address book anyway, the contacts you add on your iPad will be copied to your PC, which might be useful in future.

To synchronise your contacts, follow these steps (indicated in Figure 4.1):

1. Connect your iPad to your computer (see Chapter 2).

2. When iTunes starts, click on the name of your iPad on the left.

3. Click Info at the top of the main window.

4. Tick the box to Sync Contacts.

5. Choose the address book you'd like to sync with. On a PC, you can only sync with one address book at a time. On a Mac, you can sync with multiple address books.

6. Click the Apply button in the bottom right of the screen. iTunes will copy your contacts to your iPad.

7. You can now disconnect your iPad in the usual way (see Chapter 2).

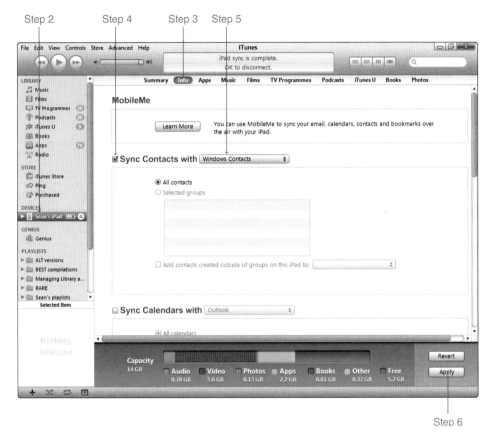

Figure 4.1

Browsing your contacts

Start the Contacts app on your iPad by tapping its icon on the Home screen. If you haven't imported any contacts yet your address book will be empty, so it won't be easy to visualise how it will look when it's finished. Take a look at Figure 4.2, which shows my final address book, to help you get your bearings.

On the left, you can see the list of contacts, grouped by the initial letter of their last name, which is shown in bold. The contacts are sorted by second name, but shown with their first name first. You can change both the order of sorting and the order in which the first and second names are displayed by going into the Settings app and tapping Contacts on the left.

If you have organised your contacts in groups using your computer, you can see these groups on your iPad by tapping Groups in the top left. To stop viewing just one group, tap Groups again and choose 'All Contacts'. You can't create or edit groups of contacts using your iPad, but if you add a new contact while you're looking at a group, the new contact will join that group.

Figure 4.2

To scroll the list of contacts, put your finger in the middle of it and drag your finger up or down. You can also flick the list to move rapidly, or tap the status bar above the list of contacts to jump to the first contact.

If you touch one of the letters in the alphabetical index on the left, you'll jump to people whose last name begins with that letter. You can also move your finger up and down this index to scroll rapidly through the address book entries.

When you tap somebody's name, their details appear on the right. You can scroll the contact page on the right up and down too, if it won't all fit in at once. If you want to email a contact's details to somebody else, tap the Share Contact button (see Figure 4.2) at the bottom of the contact's details. On iPads with cameras, you can tap the FaceTime button on a contact's page to start a video call with them (see Chapter 6). If it's someone you might want to talk to often, tap 'Add to Favourites' so you can find them more easily in the FaceTime app.

If somebody moves house or has other changes in their circumstances, you can update your address book by tapping the Edit button while their details are on screen. The process for editing a contact is similar to the process for adding one, which I'll tell you about next.

To quickly start a new email to a friend, tap their email address. Tap their real-world address to see their home in the Maps app. When the iPad with an integrated teleporter eventually ships, I expect you'll be able to materialise there in a single tap too!

Adding contacts to your iPad

Now you can see how the app is laid out, it's time to add a contact. Start by tapping the Add Contact button. This is marked with a plus sign, and is at the bottom of your list of contacts on the left-hand page of your contacts book (see Figure 4.2).

A new page in the contacts book will open, with a form for you to complete (shown in Figure 4.3). I've hidden the keyboard so that you can see the whole form, but it will open with the keyboard in view at first, so you'll need to scroll up and down to see the full form.

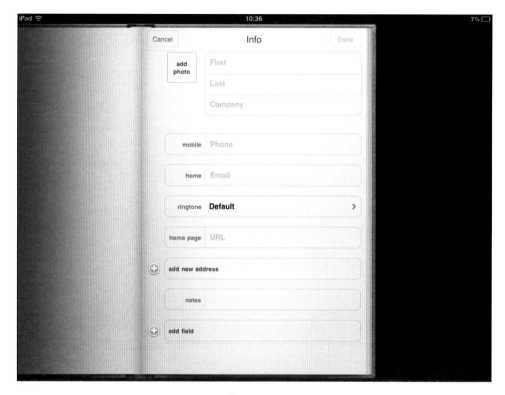

Figure 4.3

The cursor starts in the box marked 'First', which is for the person's first name. When you've finished filling in a box, either press Return on the keyboard to advance to the next box down, or tap the box you'd like to go to next. To add an address, tap Add New Address and the form will expand with space for you to enter a street, city, county, postcode and country. Once you've added one address, you can add another if you want to.

If your iPad has cameras, you can choose a ringtone for this person. This will be used to alert you when they request a FaceTime call with you (see Chapter 6).

It's easy to customise an entry to include all the information you want it to include. If you tap a label beside a box, such as 'Mobile', you can change it to something else, such as 'Home Fax'. You can also use this to change the description of the different addresses belonging to a particular person. There is a Notes box, which you can fill with any information you like, and you can scroll the form up and tap Add Field at the bottom to create extra boxes that you can label yourself.

Pay attention when you are typing in details, because the keyboard layout will change depending on what you're entering. The keyboard you're shown prioritises symbols you need most for a particular entry, such as numbers in the mobile box and the @ sign in the email box.

The Contacts app uses some conventions you've seen in other parts of the iPad, including the way you delete something in a form. If you make a mistake and want to clear a box completely, tap the box to select it and then tap the round X button inside it on the right.

You can ignore any of the boxes that you don't want to use. When you look at somebody's details later, any sections you left empty won't be shown, which minimises the amount of scrolling you need to do to see all the contact's information. Most people don't have their own website (or 'home page'), for example, so you can usually skip that box.

When you've finished adding or updating a contact, tap Done in the top right of the contact form. If you want to discard all your changes, tap Cancel in the top left.

If you have a photo of someone on your iPad (see Chapter 11), you can add it to their contact details. You will only be able to see it when you're looking at their details in the Contacts app, though, so it's only useful for reminding you who is who among your distant relatives. Tap 'add photo' to get started. If your iPad has a camera, you can take a photo of the person (see Chapter 11 for advice on taking photos). Alternatively, you can choose a photo from your iPad. You can drag the photo to centre it and use the pinch gesture (see Chapter 7) to resize it so it best fits the square space available.

Adding birthdays and anniversaries

The iPad can help you to keep track of your friends' birthdays. If you add the dates to your address book, you can use the Calendar app to see them organised in a list, or by month or week.

You can add somebody's birthday to their contact details when you're entering them for the first time, or later on by viewing their details and then tapping the Edit button.

To add a birthday, tap 'add field' and then tap 'birthday'. A box will open with a 'barrel roll' control (see Figure 4.4), which moves a bit like a fruit machine. There are 'barrels' for the date, month and year, and you change them by touching them and moving your finger up or down. You can also flick them to make them move quickly. The iPad's smart enough to know that birthdays happen every year, so I suggest you enter the year your friend was born, if you know it. When you've finished, tap outside the barrel roll to make it go away.

It is possible to add other dates, such as anniversaries, but they won't show up on the calendar. To enter another date, tap 'add field' and then tap 'date'. You can change the description of any date by tapping its label.

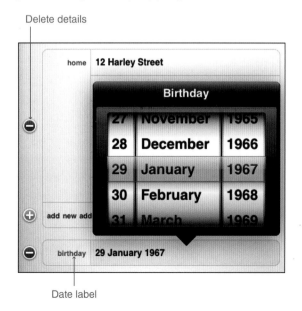

Figure 4.4

To delete a section from the contact details when you are editing them, tap the Delete Details button, which looks like a no-entry sign (see Figure 4.4). To delete all of a contact's information, tap the Delete Contact button, which appears at the bottom of a contact's details when you edit them.

Once you've added birthdays to your contacts, you can use the Calendar app to browse them by month, by week or in a list. The beauty of it is that once birthdays have been entered in Contacts, the Calendar will show them every year for you automatically. Figure 4.5 shows the month layout for the Calendar app, including my friends' birthdays. You can select a different view using the buttons at the top, and you can choose a different date using the year/month selector at the bottom of the screen.

Figure 4.5

You can use the calendar for all kinds of other things, such as reminding you to pay your credit card bill each month, planning holidays or recording when the family will be descending for dinner. To add a new event, tap the Plus button in the bottom right to open the Add Event window. You can enter the date, description, how often the event should repeat (if at all) and an alert to make sure you don't forget about it. The alert will make a sound and show on your Home screen, so that you notice it when you come back to the iPad, even if you're not there when the alert sounds.

Searching your contacts

To search for somebody in the Contacts app, tap the Search box (see Figure 4.2) and then start to type part of their name. It doesn't matter if you type their first name or surname. As you type, the iPad will filter the list of contacts underneath the search box so that it only shows those that match what you've typed so far. The moment you see the person you're looking for, tap their name to see their contact details.

To cancel the search and show the full list of results again, clear the search box. You do that by tapping the round X button inside it on the right.

One limitation with the search is that you can only find somebody by name. You can't search for everyone who lives in a particular town you're visiting, or search by phone number to see who phoned you and didn't leave a message.

The Spotlight search (see Chapter 3) will find your contacts too.

As I said at the start of this chapter, adding your contacts to your iPad means you have their details at your fingertips, and builds a good foundation for other apps on your iPad to use. In the next chapter, you'll learn how to send emails using email addresses you entered in the Contacts app. In Chapter 8, you'll learn how to search in Maps, too, so you can plot a route to somebody's house when you're visiting.

Summary

- The Contacts app is used to store information about your friends, family and acquaintances.

- The information you enter in Contacts is available to the Mail and Maps apps.

- If you already keep an address book on your computer, you might be able to synchronise with it.

- To select a contact, scroll through the list of contacts on the left.

- You can use the alphabetical index to speed up scrolling through the list or jump straight to people with a particular initial.

- You can also search by name from within Contacts, or by using the iPad's Spotlight search, or the Maps and Mail apps.

- To add a contact, tap the Add Contact button.

- You can customise each contact page, adding your own boxes of information or changing the labels against the existing ones.

- The keyboard layout changes depending on which box you are filling in.

- You can ignore any boxes you don't want to complete.

- If you have a photo of somebody on your iPad, you can add it to their contact details.

Brain training

Is your address book under control? Try this short quiz to find out.

1. The plus sign underneath your contacts list is used to:

(a) Make new friends

(b) Add a contact

(c) Scroll the contacts list to show more

(d) Tell a friend you're cross with them

2. When you're entering an email address, you can find the @ sign

(a) On the symbols keyboard (.?123)

(b) On the extra symbols keyboard (#+=)

(c) On the letters keyboard

(d) On the Home button

3. A round red sign with a white bar across it means:

(a) You can't enter anything in this box

(b) Delete a contact

(c) Delete some of a contact's information

(d) You're not allowed to call this friend

4. You can use the Calendar app to:

(a) See whose birthday is coming up this month

(b) Remind you whose anniversary it is next week

(c) Set an alert to remind you of your dental appointment

(d) Set a monthly reminder to pay the credit card bill

5. You can use Spotlight search to see:

(a) Contacts, searched by name

(b) Photos added in the Contacts app

(c) Everyone you know who lives in France

(d) All your friends who are actors

Answers

Q1 – b   **Q2** – c   **Q3** – c   **Q4** – a, c, and d   **Q5** – a
(b is only true if you've added
the anniversary separately in
the Calendar app)

Keeping in touch with friends by email

Equipment needed: An iPad with a connection to the Internet (through Wi-Fi or 3G). An email address, if you have one. Your desktop computer if you want to use it to register a new email address. A mobile phone if you want to create a new Gmail account.

Skills needed: Experience starting apps (see Chapter 3) and using the iPad keyboard (also Chapter 3). Familiarity with the Contacts app (see Chapter 4) and experience using email on other computers will be helpful but are not essential.

In this chapter, you'll learn how to send messages to your friends and read their replies using email. If you've used email on your computer, you'll find it easy to adapt to using the iPad, especially now you're an expert on the iPad keyboard. Before you can start emailing you'll need to set up the email on your iPad, but I will talk you through the steps you need to take.

If you haven't used email before, you're in for a treat! The iPad makes it easy to keep in touch with friends and family by sending them messages they can read on their computers. With email, messages wait until somebody picks them up so you don't need your friend to be using their computer at the same time as you're writing to them. It's a bit like sending a letter by post: messages are delivered and sit in the email box in the same way that letters sit on the doormat, until somebody comes home to read them. Email is easy to learn, and once you've started using it to keep in touch with your friends, you'll wonder how you ever did without it.

It doesn't matter whether your friends have iPads or not. The emails you send can be read using a computer, mobile phone or any other email-enabled device. You can read the replies on your iPad, whatever device was used to send you the message.

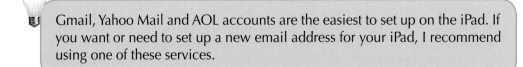

Computer engineer Ray Tomlinson of US technology company Bolt Beranek and Newman invented the use of the @ sign for email addresses in 1971. He is credited as being the first to send email across a network.

Creating an email account

To get started with email, you'll need to have an 'email account'. Similar to the way that a bank account stores your money, an email account stores your email messages. There are lots of companies that can provide you with an email account, some of them for free.

Having an email account also gives you an email address. This is used to deliver your messages to you, in the same way that your postal address is used to deliver paper mail to you (eventually). If you have an email address already, you already have an email account and don't need to set up a new one, so you can move on to 'Setting up your email account on your iPad'. If you don't already have an email account, or if you want to use a different one on your iPad, you'll need to create one first.

Although you often get an email account with your broadband subscription, you can also get one for free by registering online. Google's Gmail (**www.gmail.com**), Yahoo Mail (**http://mail.yahoo.com**) and AOL (**www.aol.com**) all operate free-of-charge 'webmail' services, so called because they enable you to use a website to read and write email. You can sign up for an email account by visiting their websites and following the instructions to create an account.

Gmail, Yahoo Mail and AOL accounts are the easiest to set up on the iPad. If you want or need to set up a new email address for your iPad, I recommend using one of these services.

You'll need to pick a password (it's best to use a jumbled up mixture of letters and numbers). You'll also be asked for a username, which is how people will address messages to you. If your username is johnwiley, for example, your email address might be johnwiley@gmail.com or johnwiley@yahoo.com. With millions of accounts already registered at these sites, you might find your preferred username is already taken, and you'll have to be creative to find one you like.

You need to have a mobile phone to register for a new email account with Google. Google sends a code to the phone, which you need to type into the website to complete your registration. However, you can register a Yahoo Mail or AOL account without having a mobile phone.

It doesn't matter whether you use your desktop computer or your iPad to visit those websites to register for your webmail account. If you want to use your iPad, skip ahead to Chapter 7 for advice on using the Safari web browser and then pick up the story here again.

Once you've registered an email address with these services, you can visit their websites and log in using your chosen username and password to read and write email.

Setting up your email account on your iPad

To get started with email, open the Mail app. It usually sits on a shelf, called the 'dock', at the bottom of the Home screen, but if you've moved it (see Chapter 12), you can find it using the Spotlight search (see Chapter 3).

When you start Mail for the first time, you'll see a set of logos showing the different email services you can set up. Although they're colourful, there's no explanation, so this screen can seem a bit unfriendly. The logos are:

● **Microsoft Exchange**: This is mainly used for business email, and it's unlikely you're using it at home. Even if you use other Microsoft software on your computer, including Windows, this is not usually the setting you need.

- **MobileMe**: You might have created a free MobileMe account to use Find My iPad (see Chapter 2), but you'll have to pay a subscription to add email to that account. You can find out more about the subscription services Apple offers and set up a free trial at **www.me.com**

- **Gmail, Yahoo and AOL**: These are free webmail accounts mentioned previously, and they're all set up in the same way.

- **Other**: This covers all other email addresses, including email accounts provided with broadband subscriptions. If you usually store your email on your desktop computer, and you can read it there even when the Internet connection is switched off, this is the option you need.

I'll show you how to set up the most common types of email account on your iPad: webmail and the mysterious 'other'.

Your iPad needs to be connected to the Internet so it can check the account details you provide are correct, and so it can download your emails. Make sure you have a good Wi-Fi or 3G connection (see Chapter 2) before proceeding.

Setting up Gmail, Yahoo and AOL webmail accounts

The iPad is programmed to recognise email accounts from Gmail, Yahoo Mail and AOL, so you don't have to type in much information. Start by tapping the logo of the email account you want to use. Figure 5.1 shows the short form you then need to complete:

- **Name**: Tap this box and then enter your full name here. The iPad will automatically use a capital letter for the first character of each word. This is the name your friends will see on any messages you send them, so they'll know to open them straight away.

- **Address**: Tap this box and enter your full email address here. It will be something like username@gmail.com, username@yahoo.com or username@aol.com. When you're typing in an email address, the @ sign is on the letters keyboard, towards the bottom right (see Figure 5.1).

- **Password**: Tap this box and then enter the password you use to log in to your webmail. Remember that the characters of the password will appear briefly on screen, so you should set up your email somewhere reasonably private. Once you've set up your email, you won't have to enter your password again.

- **Description**: The iPad will complete this automatically, but you can change it to something else if you prefer by tapping it and typing your description. It's only useful if you're planning to set up lots of email addresses on your iPad.

Figure 5.1

When you've finished, tap the Next button at the top right of the form. The iPad will then check that your information has been entered correctly and, if it has, it will give you options to synchronise your calendars and notes, as well as email. They say that a man with a watch knows the time, and a man with two watches is never sure. So if you use the calendar in Yahoo or Gmail, it makes sense to synchronise it with your iPad so that they contain the same information.

If you synchronise your notes, you will be able to read them by logging in to your webmail account. If you synchronise more than one email account with your notes, there will be new options for adding notes to your different email accounts in the Notes app. You access these options by tapping Accounts in the top left of the Notes app. When you log on to your webmail in Yahoo and AOL, your notes will be in a folder called Notes. In Gmail, they will have the label of 'Notes'. Unless you can see an immediate use for Notes synchronisation, I wouldn't bother with it.

When you've finished, tap the Save button at the top right of the form, and the iPad will start to download your emails (if you have any).

The default name in an email account on the iPad is John Appleseed. This is a reference to the legendary Johnny Appleseed (real name John Chapman), who distributed apple seedlings throughout the midwest United States. By the time he died in 1845, he owned 1,200 acres of orchard and had helped to create many more.

Setting up other email accounts

If you don't have a Gmail, AOL or Yahoo email account, then the option you are most likely to need is called 'other'. This applies if you use an email address provided to you by your broadband supplier, satellite TV company, phone company, or any other company. One of my friends buys her broadband service from her favourite supermarket, and the email address that comes with that falls under 'other' too.

Unfortunately, the 'other' option is much harder to set up than a webmail account, and you might need help from whoever set up your email account on your computer, or from your email provider's technical support.

The first form is similar to the one for webmail accounts (see Figure 5.1), so follow the guidance for webmail accounts to complete it. Your email address will probably look like yourname@yourprovider.com or yourname@yourprovider.co.uk, although you might have full stops, underscores or numbers as part of your address too.

The password is the first technical challenge, because you might not even know your email address has a password. It's usually stored in your email program so you don't have to type it in every time you download email. To find out your password, check any correspondence you have from when you set up your email account originally, or seek technical support from your email provider. If you're calling them, don't dial yet, though. There's a whole lot more they'll probably need to tell you, so read on to see what else you need to know first.

When you have completed the form, you need to tap Next at the top right. The next form (shown in Figure 5.2) carries forward some of the information you've already added but asks for additional information, which you'll need to get from your email provider.

Figure 5.2

At the top of the form are two large buttons marked IMAP and POP; these are the two different ways to access email. They work in slightly different ways, which only really matter if you're going to use multiple devices to access your email. If you read your email on POP, any other devices using the same email account won't know when you've read messages or made other changes to them. So you could read your emails on your iPad, but they would still show as new messages when you check your email on your computer. If you read your email messages on your iPad using IMAP, they will already be marked as having been read when you see them on your computer. As a rule of thumb, you can use POP if the iPad will be the only place you read your emails. If you'll be using your iPad and your computer to check your email, choose IMAP. Not all email services support both, so if in doubt, check with your email provider which of them is available to you. Tap the POP or IMAP button to select it, and it will turn blue.

You also need to provide the host name for your incoming and outgoing mail servers. These are all details you'll need to get from your email provider, but they will usually be published on its website. If you go to **www.google.com** and search for 'set up email' plus the name of your email provider, you should be able to find something helpful.

Your incoming mail server will also require a username in addition to the password you've already provided. The outgoing mail server username and password are described as optional – but it's not your choice whether you need to use them or not! If your email provider requires you to use them, it should be able to tell you what these are, but they won't be published on its website.

To scroll the form so you can see the bottom part of it underneath the keyboard, you touch the form and then drag your finger up the screen, similar to how you scrolled notes in Chapter 3. The scrolling won't work if you touch outside of the form.

When you've completed the form, tap Save at the top right, and your email will be set up.

If you have more than one email account, you can set up additional accounts by going into the Settings app and tapping Mail, Contacts, Calendars. Then, under Accounts, tap Add Account and you can now enter the details.

Sending an email

Now it's time to brighten up somebody's day by sending them an email message. You could tell them a joke, invite them round for a cuppa or just update them on the family's latest news. As long as you've got a friend's email address to hand, you're ready. If you don't know anybody else's email address you could try sending yourself an email for practice, but don't expect any surprises in the reply.

To make sure you've noted a friend's email address correctly, check it against this simple guideline: An email address always has exactly one @ sign in it, and at least one full stop after the @ sign.

To start sending an email, tap the New Email icon in the top right corner of the iPad's screen. It looks like a pen and a piece of blank paper (see Figure 5.3).

New email

Figure 5.3

Addressing your email

When you start to write a new email, a message window opens and a keyboard slides into view, so your screen looks like Figure 5.4.

The cursor starts off in the To box, which is where you enter your friend's email address. Because the iPad knows you're entering an email address, it gives you a keyboard that's designed to make that easy. The letters keyboard is enhanced with the @ sign, hyphen and underscore characters (see Figure 5.4), so you can type them without having to switch to the symbols keyboard. If the email address has numbers in it, tap .?123 to open the numbers keyboard, as you did when typing notes previously. When you finish typing an address, tap the Return key, and a rounded box will appear around the email address.

Pick from contacts

Underscore

Delete

@ sign

Hyphen

Figure 5.4

If the person you want to email is in your contacts and you've entered their email address there, you don't have to type it twice. Tap the blue + sign (see Figure 5.4) to pick an address from your contacts without leaving the Mail app.

It's possible to send the same message to several people at the same time, so after you've entered an email address your cursor will stay in the To box so that you can add any additional email addresses there, either by typing them or by selecting them from your contacts.

As well as adding multiple recipients in the To box, there are two other ways you can address an email to somebody:

● **Cc**: This sends someone a courtesy copy of the email. This is often used when you want to keep someone informed about the conversation you're having but you don't expect them to get involved in replying. Everyone who gets a copy of the email can see the email address of everyone who has been sent the message using To or Cc.

● **Bcc**: This works like Cc except that the B stands for 'blind', so nobody else can see that this recipient has received a copy of the email. Those who receive a Bcc copy can still see the To and the Cc recipients, though. If several people receive a Bcc copy, they can't see each other's email address either. You can use this if you're emailing people who don't know each other and who might not want you to give out their email addresses to each other.

If you want to use Cc or Bcc to address somebody, tap the Cc/Bcc box and separate rows will open for Cc and Bcc. You can then tap these and enter the email addresses or contacts into them.

If you need to delete an email address from the email, tap that name or email address and then tap the Delete key on the keyboard (see Figure 5.4).

When you finish completing a box, you can tap Return to advance to the next box. If you want to Cc or Bcc someone, you'll have to tap the Cc/Bcc box, though, because tapping Return in the To box will skip over it and take you straight to the email subject.

Writing your email message

Once you've addressed your email, you can craft your message. There are two parts to this: the subject line and the message itself.

The subject line of the email is a short description of what it's about. It helps people to tell different email conversations apart and find messages they need more easily. In most email programs, the first thing people will see is your name and the email subject, and they'll have to open the email to see the rest. It's a good idea to have a clear, concise and meaningful description that will uniquely identify your message. Something like 'Planning August theatre outing' is much more useful than 'Chat', and emails with blank subject lines can be easily overlooked. On the iPad, the subject line is positioned between the addressees and the main message area, in common with other email programs you might have used.

Underneath the subject box is a large box in which you write your email message. You write your message in the same way you write notes (see Chapter 3), and the keyboard reverts to the same layout as in the Notes app. The Auto-text, selection, copy, cut, paste and editing features all work in the same way as they do in Notes.

When you've finished composing your message, tap the Send button at the top right of the email form. If you have an Internet connection, your message is immediately sent to the recipient. Otherwise, you'll see an error message, but your email will be stored on your iPad and sent next time you open the Mail app and do have an Internet connection.

If you decide to abandon the email, tap Cancel at the top left. You'll have the option to save a draft of the email, which means it won't be sent but will be kept in your draft folder so you can edit and send it later. If you delete the draft, the email will be permanently deleted.

Cheekily, Apple puts a line at the end of each message that says, "Sent from my iPad" to make sure all your friends think about buying one too. This is the email 'signature', which concludes every message you send. You can change it to something else if you prefer, such as your full name and favourite quotation. To edit this, go into the Settings app, tap Mail, Contacts, Calendars and then tap Signature.

Email works a bit differently on the iPad to the way it works on a computer, so it might take a few minutes to get the hang of it. Once you have, though, you can send messages from anywhere you take your iPad and have an Internet connection. Give it a go!

Reading your emails

After you've sent out a few messages, hopefully you'll get a few replies. If your iPad is set up with the same email account as your desktop computer, you might already have a stream of messages flowing in.

The Mail app probably looks a bit different to the email programs you've used before, so it might be hard to see at a glance how you do things like read an email, reply to one or delete one you don't need any more.

When you go into the Mail app, it will download your latest emails, and you'll see a screen like the one shown in Figure 5.5, if you're using your iPad landscape. If you rotate your iPad, you'll see just one email at a time. That's useful if you're reading long emails, but the landscape format stops you having to tap so often to open new messages, so I'll stick to that in this chapter.

The column on the left shows a list of the messages in your inbox, with the most recent at the top. You can scroll the message list up and down by putting your finger on it and dragging it up or down, or by flicking it. To jump back to the top, tap the status bar above the list (see Figure 5.5).

The number in brackets at the top of the list of messages tells you how many unread messages you have in your inbox.

Each email has a summary box in the message list detailing who sent it, the time (today) or date (before today) the email was sent, the subject line, and a short snippet from the start of the message. Unread emails have a blue bobble beside them, so you can quickly identify them. When you tap the email's summary box, the email's entry in the message list is coloured blue and the full email opens on the right and can be scrolled up and down in the usual way.

If the email is part of an ongoing conversation, its entry in the message list will include a number in a black box to indicate how many messages there are in that conversation, or 'thread' (see the first email in Figure 5.5, which is part of a thread with two messages). When you tap the email in the message list, the list will change to show only the previous emails you've received with the same subject line. To see all your messages again, just tap the Inbox button in the top left.

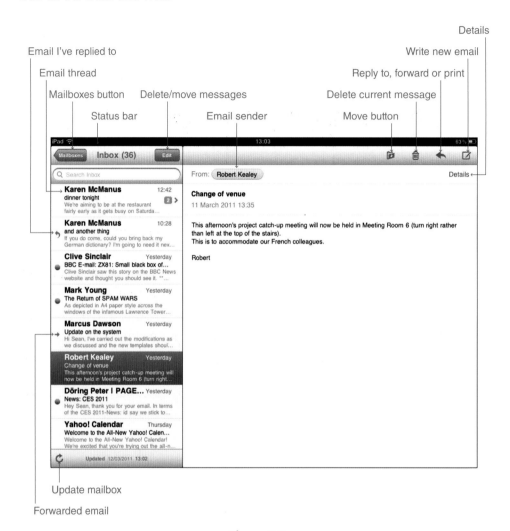

Figure 5.5

There are several things you can do with an email once you've selected it in the message list (see Figure 5.5):

● **Add the sender as a contact**: Tap the sender's name and you can create a new contact for them, or add their email address to an existing contact. Because you can choose email recipients from your contacts list, this can make it easier to send emails to that person in future.

- **Reply to or forward the email**: Tap the arrow in the top right, and you can choose to reply to the email or forward it to somebody else. After that, the process is similar to writing a new email. If you reply to a message, a curved left arrow appears beside it in the message list. If you forward a message, a right-pointing arrow appears.

- **Print**: If you have a compatible printer, tap the arrow in the top right to find the print option.

- **Delete/Archive email**: Tap the dustbin icon in the top right and the email you're reading will be moved to the Trash folder. If you have a Gmail address, the dustbin icon is changed to a filing cabinet. When you tap it, your email is archived, which means it vanishes from your inbox but is still available if you need it later.

- **Mark as unread**: If you read a message but want to leave it marked as unread, tap Details at the top right of the message and then tap Mark as Unread.

- **See all the recipients**: Tap Details at the top, to see who else got a copy of the email.

- **View an attachment**: Scroll to the end of an email message to see any attachments it has. Tap the attachment and it will open. When you've finished, tap Done in the top left. If necessary, tap the document first to make the Done button appear. The iPad can also play audio or video attachments.

You can also delete an email by swiping left or right over its entry in the message list and then tapping the Delete button that appears in the message list. If you don't want to delete, tap elsewhere in the message list.

Managing email folders

So far, everything you've seen has taken place in the Inbox, the folder where new emails are filed. There are other mailboxes you can use, which include:

- **Drafts**: If you abandon an email halfway through writing it but save it so you can finish and send later, this is where you'll find it.

- **Sent**: This folder stores the emails you have sent to others.

- **Trash**: This folder contains emails you have deleted.

- **Bulk Mail or Spam**: Where offered, this folder contains email that your email provider believes is junk email. It's worth checking this folder from time to time in case your email provider has moved a real message to this mailbox by mistake.

To access all of your folders, tap Mailboxes in the top left of the screen (see Figure 5.5). You can then choose a folder from the list, which might look similar to Figure 5.6. If you have multiple email accounts, the inboxes for the accounts are all listed at the top, and then you need to tap the account names further down the screen to find the individual folders.

Figure 5.6

Unfortunately, you can't create new folders on the iPad, although if you use a service like Yahoo Mail or Gmail, you can create new folders or labels by logging in to your webmail account using the web browser on your iPad or your computer. These new folders will then appear on the iPad. If you have set up different named folders in your webmail account, you can move a message between them easily. When you're reading an email, tap the Move button (indicated in Figure 5.5) and then choose a folder.

To move or delete lots of messages in one go, tap the Edit button at the top of the message list. Then tap the messages you'd like to select, and tap Delete or Move at the bottom of the column. If you're moving messages, tap the folder you'd like to move to. Tap Cancel at the top of the message list if you change your mind.

Searching your emails

You can use the Spotlight search to find emails, or you can use the search built into Mail. Whichever you use, it can only search for people an email was received from or sent to, or the subject line. That's another reason good subject lines are important.

The search built into Mail works in a similar way to the one in Notes (see Figure 5.7). You tap the Search box at the top left, and then type the name or word you're looking for. Matching emails appear underneath and you can tap any of them to read them. To cancel the search, tap the Cancel button (see Figure 5.7). To clear the search box and start looking for something else, tap the X in the circle in the search box.

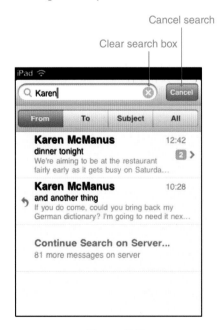

Figure 5.7

Downloading new emails

Your email messages are stored in a mailbox managed by your email provider. Your iPad then downloads these emails to its internal storage over the Internet. It starts by downloading the most recent 50 emails (you can change this number in the Settings app) and then you can tap Load More Messages at the bottom of the message list to download another batch.

Whenever you go into the Mail app, your iPad checks for any new email messages in your mailbox. At any time you like, you can make it check for more new messages by tapping the Update Mailbox button at the bottom of the message list (indicated in Figure 5.5).

Some types of email account (including Yahoo Mail) can automatically push new messages to your iPad shortly after they arrive in your mailbox, as long as you have an Internet connection. This means you get messages almost as soon as they're available, but the drawback is that it runs down your battery more quickly.

For accounts that can't push messages to you, the iPad can automatically check at regular intervals (15, 30 or 60 minutes) to see whether you've had any new messages. Again, this is something that will run down your battery more quickly, and it isn't necessary if you won't be checking what's been downloaded for some time anyway.

By default, the iPad is set to allow emails to be pushed to your iPad where possible, but it doesn't have regular checking activated. You can change this by going into the Settings app and tapping Mail, Contacts, Calendars. You can also switch off the sounds you hear whenever you send or receive an email, by editing the General settings.

To conserve battery life, it's a good idea to check email manually and just download it when you open the Mail app or tap the Update button.

The Mail icon on the Home screen has a red circle in the corner of it showing how many unread messages you have in your main inbox.

Summary

- You can use the iPad to read emails sent using any kind of device or computer. Emails from your iPad can be read using any email-compatible device, too.

- The Mail app is used for reading and writing emails.

- The easiest way to set up email is to use a free email account from Yahoo, Google or AOL.

- Use the Other option to set up most other types of email account, including those typically provided by broadband suppliers.

- You can pick people from your contacts to send an email to.

- To send someone a copy of an email, use Cc. To send someone a copy of an email but hide their details from everyone else receiving it, use Bcc.

- Use a clear and specific subject line.

- To add the same text to the end of all your outgoing messages, such as your full name, edit the email signature in your Settings app.

- The message list shows a short preview of the messages in your mailbox. Tap one to read it in full.

- A threaded email is one that is part of a discussion. Tap it in the message list to see the previous emails with the same subject line.

- Tap the curved arrow in the top right to reply to an email, forward it or print it.

- When you receive an email, you can add its sender to your contacts so it's easier to email them in future.

- You can move emails between different folders.

- The search will find emails by sender name, recipient or subject line.

- Some types of email account can push emails to your iPad when they arrive. Your iPad can also check for emails regularly. To save battery power, turn off the automatic updating of email.

Brain training

At the end of that bumper project, relax with a short quiz to see how much you've remembered.

1. Which of these is a valid email address?

(a) fred@example@com

(b) www.example.com

(c) fred.bloggs@examplecom

(d) freddieboy@example.com

2. To set up an AOL account on your iPad, you need to know:

(a) Your username

(b) Your incoming and outgoing server details

(c) Your password

(d) Whether it is IMAP or POP

3. A good subject line might be:

(a) Stuff

(b) Hello

(c) Thought you'd like this

(d) Booking tickets to see The Australian Pink Floyd

4. An email thread is:

(a) A group of sent messages

(b) An email message that's as long as a piece of string

(c) A group of emails with the same subject line

(d) A folder of messages

5. To find a party invitation email in your inbox, search using:

(a) The name of someone else who got a copy of the invitation

(b) The name of the pub mentioned in the message

(c) The word 'birthday', which was in the subject line

(d) The name of the person who sent you the message

Answers

Q1 – d   **Q2** – a and c   **Q3** – d   **Q4** – c   **Q5** – a, c and d

Using FaceTime for video calls

6

Equipment needed: An iPad with built-in cameras and a Wi-Fi connection. A friend with a FaceTime-compatible device and the FaceTime app.

Skills needed: Familiarity with the Contacts app (see Chapter 4) is helpful.

If you have a first generation iPad, which doesn't have built-in cameras, then I'm afraid you can't use FaceTime.

Skip ahead to the next chapter! When Apple launched the second generation of the iPad (known as the iPad 2), it added video calling. For many years, technology like this – the ability to see who you're phoning as you speak to them – was the stuff of science fiction. In recent years you might have used a webcam with your computer to have a video chat with people over the Internet, but that meant you only ever got to see people sitting in front of their computers. The iPad, with its two built-in cameras, makes this kind of technology much more portable, so you can chat to people from all over your house as well as many other places.

You can't chat just anywhere, though: even if you have a 3G compatible iPad, a Wi-Fi connection needs to be available for you to be able to use the video-calling feature. As you know, these are often provided in cafés and holiday resorts, so it's usually easy to get connected for a chat. The upside of using Wi-Fi is that it's usually free, which, oddly, makes video calls cheaper than many phone calls.

The app used for video calling is FaceTime, and the iPad comes with this already installed on it. The person you want to talk to must also have FaceTime, but they don't necessarily need to have an iPad; they may have FaceTime if they have an iPhone, an iPod Touch or an Apple Mac computer, as FaceTime software is also available for these. Not all versions of these devices support FaceTime, but if the device has a camera on the front, it should work with FaceTime. FaceTime is sold separately for the Apple Mac, but comes preinstalled on other devices.

FaceTime is a fantastic feature of the iPad. It's strange, but after a video chat you really do feel like you've met someone. It feels completely different to a phone call.

Tap the FaceTime app on your Home screen to get started.

If you don't have the FaceTime app on your Home screen, your iPad probably isn't compatible with it. Remember, you need one of the newer iPads with built-in cameras for FaceTime to work.

Logging in to FaceTime

To use FaceTime, you need to log in using your Apple ID. This is the same email address and password combination you used when you set up your iPad, and which you'll use to download music and video (see Chapter 9) and apps (see Chapter 12) from Apple's store. If you don't have an Apple ID, tap the Create New Account button.

If a friend wants to set up a FaceTime call with you, they'll need to use your email address. The FaceTime app will ask you which email address you want people to use to contact you. If you're happy to use the same email address as you use for your Apple ID, just tap Next in the top right. Otherwise, tap the email address itself and you can delete it and type in a new address. Tap Next when you've finished.

You can also add additional email addresses for yourself in the FaceTime section of the Settings app. This is useful if you have multiple email addresses and friends might try to contact you using any of them.

When you enter an email address for FaceTime, you might need to verify it is yours. If so, Apple will send you an email with a link in it. You'll need to check your email using your computer and click the link Apple sends you. This proves to Apple that you own the email address, and acts as a security measure for FaceTime because it stops people from using email addresses they don't own. You won't need to verify your email address if the email address you enter is already linked to your Apple ID or is one that you have already set up in the Mail app (see Chapter 5).

You can leave your iPad signed in to FaceTime so that you don't have to enter your email address and password the next time you want to use it. If you want to log out for some reason (perhaps to enable someone else to use FaceTime with their own ID), you can do that by going into the Settings app.

Starting a FaceTime call

The first shock you get when you start the FaceTime app is that you see your own face filling the screen (see Figure 6.1). That's me, by the way. Nice to meet you.

Down the right hand side of the screen is a list of people to call. If you tap Recents at the bottom, you can see people you've recently called, tried to call or received calls from. The Favourites section shows you people you've labelled as 'favourites' within FaceTime or the Contacts app. Tap Contacts to see people in your address book, which is shared with the Contacts and Mail apps. This is a great time saver, because it means you don't have to enter a friend's email address again if you've already done so in Contacts or Mail.

If you haven't added the person you want to talk to as a contact in your iPad, you need to do that before you can call them. FaceTime makes it easy to add a contact by tapping the Add Contact button in the top right corner of the screen (see Figure 6.1). As a bare minimum, you should add their first name, last name and the email address or iPhone phone number they use for FaceTime. You don't need to enter any further details to use FaceTime but, if you wish, you can flesh out your contact's profile with more detail so it's there for you to refer to in the Contacts app. For advice on completing your contact's details, and a refresher on how the Contacts app works on the iPad, see Chapter 4.

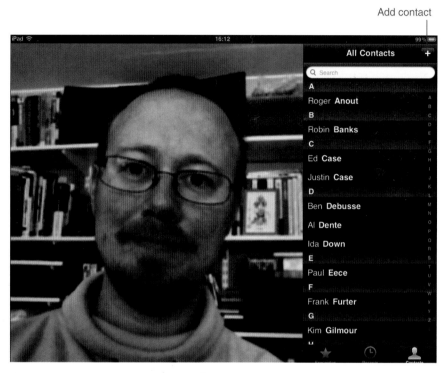

Figure 6.1

To find the contact you want to call, you can scroll the contacts list by touching it and dragging your finger up and down, or you can use the search box at the top of the screen. Tap somebody's name and you will see full contact details for them. This provides you with three particularly useful options:

● **Add to favourites**: Since not everyone in your address book will have FaceTime, you can save yourself a lot of time by adding those who do have it to your Favourites list. You can then see a list of only these people by tapping Favourites at the bottom of the screen.

● **Edit**: To make a FaceTime call to your friend, you will need to contact them using the email address or phone number they have registered with Apple for use in FaceTime. That might not be the same address they use for correspondence, so, if necessary, you'll need to tap the Edit button in the top right and add their FaceTime email address or phone number to their contact details.

● **Start a FaceTime call**: There's no big button to press! To start a FaceTime call, just tap the email address your friend uses for FaceTime, or their iPhone phone number.

When you tap an email address or phone number, FaceTime will attempt to call your friend and you'll hear a simulated phone ringing sound. Your friend will see a message on screen and hear an alert sound if they have alerts enabled. When your friend answers, you'll see their face on the screen.

If the iPad tells you almost immediately that someone you're trying to call isn't available for FaceTime, it's probably because FaceTime doesn't know that email address. Check you've got the right email address and that you've spelled it correctly.

Talking to a friend with FaceTime

During a call, the FaceTime screen looks like Figure 6.2. Most of the screen is filled with the video of your friend, but overlaid on this are a few controls as well.

In the top left is a small picture showing what your friend is seeing of you. If this is in the way of something you want to see in your friend's video, you can touch it and drag it to another corner of the screen, but you can't get rid of it. Most of the time, you can just leave it alone. It's worth keeping an eye on this from time to time to make sure that you're not covering the camera with your thumb, or giving your friend an unflattering view up your nostrils. The camera on the front of your iPad is opposite the Home button, so it's best to hold the iPad near its corners or to stand it up to avoid blocking the camera.

At the bottom of the screen are three buttons. On the left is a Mute button, which is probably more acceptable in business than personal use. It seems a bit rude to stop someone you've called from hearing what you're saying, but if you need a moment of privacy, this button will give you it. The images continue, however, so don't rely on the Mute button if your friend can lip-read!

Mute

End call

Swap cameras

Image courtesy of Kim Gilmour

Figure 6.2

On the right is a button to swap between using the cameras on the front and back of your iPad. Most of the time, you'll want to use the front-facing camera, so that you can see your friend on the screen and they can see you looking at them on the screen. Sometimes you might want to share something that's going on, however, such as the view from your window, or a birthday party. Tap the Swap Cameras button, and Face-Time will use the camera on the back of your iPad instead of the front. That means your friend will be able to see whatever you point your iPad at, and you'll still be able to see what they're seeing and their reaction to it on your screen. The back camera is in a corner near the Sleep/Wake button – take care with how you hold your iPad when using the back camera, to make sure you don't cover the lens. To revert to using the front-facing camera, simply tap the Swap Cameras button again.

If you want to move around as you talk, try not to move too quickly. The image can become blocky and indistinct if you move too fast, so it's best to prop your iPad up on the desk if you're just chatting, or move the iPad around slowly if you're giving your friend a tour.

> Remember that you need a good Wi-Fi connection to use FaceTime. If you move too far away from the Wi-Fi hotspot while you're chatting, your connection might break up, resulting in poor quality sound and video.

If you rotate your iPad, the view on the other person's screen will also rotate, so that your friend always sees things the right way up.

You can break off the video chat to look something up on your iPad while you're still talking. You could look up someone's address in the Contacts app, for example, if you're arranging to meet at their house later. Press the Home button and you will go to the Home screen, where you can start another app. The video your friend sees will be paused, and your own screen will be filled with the Home screen and whatever apps you use, so you won't see any video either. You can still hear and speak to each other, though. When you're ready to go back into FaceTime, tap the green bar at the top of the screen where the iPad says 'Touch to resume FaceTime'.

When it's time to finish the call, tap the End Call button in the middle of the screen at the bottom.

After you've had a successful call with someone, a video camera icon also appears beside their email address or phone number when you view their contact details in the FaceTime app, which is a helpful reminder of which one they use for FaceTime when you want to talk to them again in future.

Receiving a FaceTime call

Your friends can request FaceTime chats with you too. If your iPad has been muted (see Chapter 2), you won't hear anything, but otherwise you will hear your iPad make an alert sound. If you've specified a ringtone for your friend in the Contacts app (see Chapter 4), your iPad will use that sound to let you know who's calling. You'll also see a message telling you who would like to have a FaceTime chat with you. There are two buttons: Decline, which will block the call; and Accept, which will start the call straight away.

If you don't want to be interrupted by FaceTime requests, you can turn FaceTime off in the Settings app.

Summary

- The FaceTime app enables you to have video calls with friends.
- It is available for the iPad, iPhone, iPod Touch and Mac computers (but not for the first generation of the iPad, which does not have built-in cameras).
- To use FaceTime, you need to have a Wi-Fi connection.
- You log in to FaceTime using your Apple ID.
- People contact you using the email address you have entered in FaceTime.
- You need to add someone to your contacts before you can call them.
- To start a call, tap someone's email address or iPhone phone number in the FaceTime app.
- You can swap between the front or back camera when using FaceTime.
- If someone wants to have a call with you, you'll see a message on your iPad's screen.
- In the Settings app, you can turn off Face-Time or add additional email addresses that people can use to contact you.

Brain training

How did you get on with FaceTime? Find out with this quick quiz.

1. **You can use FaceTime to call someone with:**

(a) A second generation iPad (iPad 2)

(b) A first generation iPad

(c) A Windows PC

(d) An Apple Mac computer

2. **People contact you on FaceTime using:**

(a) Your iPad's serial number

(b) Your phone number

(c) Any email address you have

(d) Any email address you've entered in FaceTime

3. **To use Face Time on your iPad, you need to have:**

(a) An iPad with cameras

(b) A 3G Internet connection

(c) A Wi-Fi Internet connection

(d) A Mac computer

4. **To turn off the video but keep the audio working in a FaceTime chat, you:**

(a) Tap the Mute button

(b) Press the Home button

(c) Tap the Swap Cameras button

(d) Tap the End Call button

5. **To make sure your FaceTime calls go well, you should:**

(a) Check you're calling the right email address

(b) Keep your fingers away from the camera lens

(c) Make sure your iPad is not muted so you hear the ringtone

(d) Comb your hair

Answers

Q1 – a and d   **Q2** – d   **Q3** – a and c   **Q4** – b   **Q5** – a, b, c and d

Browsing the web

7

Equipment needed: An iPad with an Internet connection (Wi-Fi or 3G).

Skills needed: Experience of editing text and using the iPad keyboard (see Chapter 3).

One of the best features of the iPad is the ease with which you can browse the Internet. From the comfort of your sofa, a cafe, or even in bed, you can look at family photos on Facebook, book your holiday, do your banking or search for the answer to pretty much any question. Almost everything you can do online with a conventional computer, you can do with the iPad.

I said *almost* anything. One thing the iPad doesn't support is Flash, which is a format used for playing animations, music and video on the Internet. Nobody will mourn the loss of those irritating splat-the-monkey adverts you sometimes see on websites, but if you like to play games online, you might find some of them don't work on the iPad. Video sharing website YouTube still works (see Chapter 10) but you won't be able to play the video and audio on some websites. For most people, the lack of Flash isn't a real problem, though.

To get started, make sure you have a web connection (see Chapter 2). The app you use for viewing web pages on the iPad (known as the 'web browser') is called Safari. You can find it on the dock at the bottom of your Home screen, on the left. If you've moved it (see Chapter 12), you can use the Spotlight search to find it too.

If you are using a 3G connection, don't worry about how long you're connected. It's not like a phone call where you're charged by the minute. You only pay for the content you download, so it's the amount of content you need to be aware of, not the amount of time you spend on it. It doesn't matter how long you spend reading a web page before going to another one.

In this chapter, I'll show you how to get the most from Safari. You'll build on the skills you acquired in using the keyboard and editing text in Chapter 3, and on your experience of using the Internet on other computers. If you don't already know how to use the Internet, you can download a free chapter from *Social Networking for the Older and Wiser* at **www.sean.co.uk** for a quick introduction.

Start the Safari app, and we're ready to go!

There is small risk that somebody could intercept data you send over the Internet when you're using public Wi-Fi, so it's best to avoid online shopping, banking or other sensitive activities when you're using Wi-Fi in public places like cafés or hotels.

Entering a website address

The Safari browser looks much like a browser on a desktop computer, so there will be few surprises when the Safari app starts. At the top, you'll see two boxes: one for the website address, and the other for searching the web (see Figure 7.1).

To go straight to a particular website, you need to tell the browser its website address. This usually starts with 'www.' followed by a word or phrase, followed by a domain extension such as .com, .co.uk or .org. Website addresses you've probably used before include **www.bbc.co.uk** and **www.google.com**. These short addresses take you to the website's home page, which is designed to welcome new visitors.

Every different page of content on the website has its own, longer website address too. You could type the longer address in to jump straight to a particular article on a website, but it's usually easier to go to the website's home page and then click some links to find what you want, or to use the search engine to go there.

To enter a website address on the iPad, start by tapping the address field at the top of the screen (see Figure 7.1). The keyboard will appear so that you can type in the website address.

It is often fine if you leave out the 'www.' at the start, as this is often automatically inserted, so you can save time by just typing in 'bbc.co.uk', for example.

If you mistype anything in the address field, you can edit what you've typed. Tap and hold in the address field, and the magnifying glass will appear so you can easily position your insertion point. You can then type missing letters or use the keyboard's Delete key to remove characters. You can also paste a website address, if you've copied it from an email or the Notes app, for example. Before you paste a new website address into the address field, clear the old one by tapping the Clear Address Field button (the X) in the right of the address field.

When you've finished typing your website address, tap the Go key, which is where the Return key normally is on the right of the keyboard.

There are a couple of features that are designed to make it easier to enter website addresses. Firstly, when you're typing in a website address, the keyboard includes the symbols you're most likely to need, and incorporates a .com key. You can use that key to add .com to the end of your address, or another popular domain extension (such as .net, .edu, .eu, .org, .co.uk, .uk or .ie). To add .com, just tap the key normally. To add one of the others, tap the .com key and hold it. A bubble will appear showing those other domain extensions (see Figure 7.1). When it does, slide your finger over to the domain extension you want and then release your finger. This works similar to the way you chose accented letters in the Notes app (see Chapter 3).

Bookmarks bar   Address field   Clear address field   Search field

.com key   Domain extensions

PC Wisdom is ©2000-2011 by John Wiley & Sons, Inc.

Figure 7.1

> ⚠️ The additional domain extensions in the bubble include both .co.uk and .uk. Most of the time, you probably need to choose .co.uk but .uk is the one that's highlighted initially. Make sure you pick the right one!

The other way that Safari helps you to enter websites is that it will suggest websites you might like to visit while you type. These suggestions are drawn from sites you've previously visited, or those you have bookmarked (see later in this chapter). The suggestions appear underneath the address field, as you can see in Figure 7.1.

Each suggestion has the title of the page in bold, with its full website address underneath in grey. If you're returning to a website, keep an eye on these suggestions. The moment the iPad knows where you're going, you can tap a suggestion to go there straight away.

Don't spoil the surprise! If you've used the iPad to book a romantic getaway or order flowers, you might be rumbled if your partner sees the websites you've visited. To remove the history of websites you've visited, go into your Settings app and tap Safari. You can then clear the history (of visited websites), cookies (small files websites use to recognise you when you return) and cache (files from a website stored on your iPad to speed up return visits). You can also clear the history by tapping the bookmarks icon in Safari (see later in this chapter).

You can also find websites by using the search field on the right. While you type, Google will suggest phrases that match what you're typing. If one of them is what you want, you can stop typing and just tap it. If not, when you've finished typing, tap the Search key on the keyboard. You'll find it in place of the Return key.

Zooming the page

Many websites were designed for much bigger screens than the iPad, or use text that is too small to read comfortably. In Chapter 2, you learned about a way you can use the accessibility settings to zoom the whole screen. This feature is ideal for people who have impaired vision, because it enables them to enlarge the iPad's onscreen buttons as well as the content. There is a drawback, in that it sometimes moves the controls off the screen, so you might have to do more scrolling around to find them again.

If you just want to see part of a web page more clearly, the zoom accessibility controls are excessive, so you have a choice of two alternative ways you can enlarge just the content of a web page. Perhaps the simplest is to double-tap a column of text, and it will be enlarged to fill the width of the screen. Double-tap again, and the screen will zoom out again so you can pick another column of text to zoom in on.

There's also a gesture used for zooming, called the pinch. It works like this: you put two fingers on the screen, near the content you want to enlarge (see Figure 7.2). You then move those fingers apart, and the screen will zoom in on the space between your fingers (see Figure 7.3). People usually use the pointing finger and thumb of the same hand, but if this is uncomfortable for you, you can use two fingers from different hands.

PC Wisdom is ©2000-2011 by John Wiley & Sons, Inc.

Figure 7.2

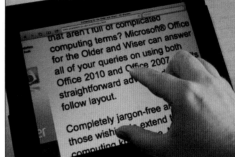

PC Wisdom is ©2000-2011 by John Wiley & Sons, Inc.

Figure 7.3

The pinch is also used for enlarging photos (see Chapter 11). Practise it and you'll find it gives you a lot of control over what you see on your iPad screen.

Pictures can become indistinct when zoomed in too far, but the text of a web page will sharpen when you remove your fingers from the screen.

To go back to the web page's original size, perform the pinch in reverse. Start with your fingers apart on the screen, and then bring them close together. If you shrink the page too far, it will snap back to fit the screen when you release your fingers.

Scrolling the page

A web page will often spill off the available screen area, especially when you zoom in.

To scroll the page so you can see a different part of it, put your finger anywhere on it and then drag it across the iPad's screen. As you move your finger up or down the screen, the web page will scroll in that direction. If the web page is wide or has been zoomed in, you can also scroll sideways.

While you are scrolling, a thin scrollbar appears at the right and/or bottom of the screen to give you a visual clue of which part of the page you're looking at. The longer the line, the more of the page's total height or width you're looking at. The position of the line also tells you where you are on the page.

For example, Figure 7.4 shows a page I've zoomed in, which has two scrollbars. The one at the bottom shows me that I'm looking at about 80% of the page's width, and I'm looking at the left side. The scrollbar along the right side of the screen shows me that I'm looking at only about 10% of the page's height, and I'm nearly halfway down the page.

On a desktop computer, you might be used to seeing a scrollbar at the side of the screen all the time to tell you there's more to see. You don't get that on the iPad, so it's a good idea to try scrolling the page to see what you might be missing.

You can use the flick gesture you learned in Chapter 3 to quickly move in any direction on the web page, but it's particularly useful for zipping through pages that are several screenfuls deep.

The navigation options for a website are usually at the top of the screen. When you finish reading a page, you can jump to the top of it by tapping the status bar, indicated in Figure 7.4, so that you can find its links.

You can often see more of a web page by rotating the iPad. Try the landscape and portrait orientations to see which you find most comfortable for reading.

Back

Forward

Multiple windows

Status bar

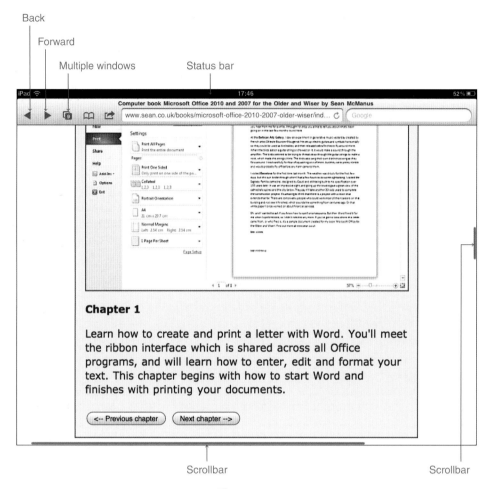

Scrollbar

Scrollbar

Figure 7.4

Using links on websites

Now that you know how to view a website, it's time to look at how you can inter-act with it. As you probably know from your experience with desktop computers, web pages are connected together using links. Links can be text, in which case they are usually underlined, or they can be pictures, in which case they might look like buttons.

To use a link on a website, whether it's text or an image, you just tap it. With all the pinching and scrolling going on, you might think there's a danger of touching the wrong part of the screen and being taken away to a page you didn't want. That doesn't happen: the iPad doesn't decide you've tapped a link until you remove your finger again; if you've moved your finger in between, it guesses you intended to scroll. If you put two or more fingers on the screen at once, it won't select a link for either of them, because you can't choose more than one link at the same time.

Web pages on the iPad look the same as they do on a desktop computer, but there's one significant difference. On a PC, your mouse cursor can be over a link without you clicking it, and this is sometimes used to make a menu appear on the screen. On the iPad, your finger is either touching the screen or it isn't. On a well designed website it should still be obvious where the links are, but you might have to tap first to open menus that normally pop up automatically when you're using a desktop computer.

Like a desktop browser, your iPad is able to take you back to the previous page you looked at, or forward again after you've gone back. The Back and Forward buttons are in the top left of the browser, as indicated in Figure 7.4.

Entering information into websites

Often you'll want to enter information into a website, such as your username and password, or perhaps your address if you are shopping online. The way you enter information into a website is similar to the way that you added information in the Settings app or addressed emails, but there are a couple of things to look out for.

As you might expect, you tap a text entry box to bring up a keyboard so you can type something into it. The first thing to look out for is that the keyboard layout can change depending on what you're typing in. Some websites tell the iPad you're entering an email address so that you get a keyboard with an @ sign within easy reach, for example, but not all websites do this.

The second thing to look out for is that the Return key on the keyboard is replaced with a Go key. Previously, you used the Return key to move to the next box that you need to complete but here, tapping the Go key submits your form as if you'd tapped the Submit button for the form. If you tap the Go key before you've finished filling in all the boxes, you might have to go back to the beginning and complete the form all over again.

To enter information into other boxes, therefore, tap the box rather than tapping the Go key. While the keyboard is in view, you can still scroll the underlying web page to make sure you can complete all the information you need to.

To select a radio button (a radio button is a round one that is used to choose one of several options), tick a checkbox or choose from a pulldown menu, just tap it. In the case of a pulldown menu, the menu will open so that you can tap your option.

If you're entering sensitive information into the website, such as credit card details, make sure you're using a secure web page. To check, look at the web page title. It's in the grey bar at the top of the screen, immediately underneath the time in the status bar. A secure web page has a tiny padlock icon to the left of the page title. Don't be tricked by any padlocks in the web page content. If it's not in the grey bar at the top of your browser, it doesn't count.

Browsing multiple websites at the same time

Safari enables you to have nine web pages open at the same time. This can be useful when you're shopping online and comparing the offers from different websites, if you're trying to coordinate flight bookings in one window with hotel reservations in another, or even if you just want to take a short deviation and read something such as an encyclopaedia article before continuing to read a news report.

Sometimes when you click a link, it will open in a new window of its own accord, but you can choose to open any link in a new window. To do that, tap and hold the link until a menu pops up (see Figure 7.5).

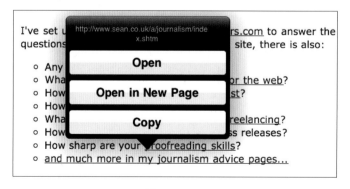

Figure 7.5

At the top of the menu that opens when you tap and hold a link, you can see the website address the link goes to. You can open this menu if you're not sure about where a link will take you and you want to check its destination before you follow it.

The menu's options are:

● **Open**: Tap this to open the link in the current window (that is, to replace the page that is open with the new one). This is the same thing that happens if you just tap the link, but it gives you a chance to check where it will go first.

● **Open in New Page**: Tap this to open the link in a new window.

● **Copy**: Tap this to copy the link's website address. If you want to send somebody the link, you could use this to take a copy of its address and then paste it into an email in the Mail app. There's an easier way to send somebody a link, though, which I'll show you later.

● **Do nothing**: This isn't actually an option on the menu, but if you tap outside the menu, it will close again. That's good to know if you open the menu by accident.

If you want to see all the windows you have open, tap the Multiple Windows button at the top of the browser (this looks like two overlapping boxes and is indicated in Figure 7.4). If more than one window is open, this icon will have a number in it to tell you how many are open. When you tap this button, you'll be shown screenshots of all the websites you have open (see Figure 7.6). From here, you have three options:

● **Return to a website**: To go back to a particular website, tap its screenshot and the window will fill the iPad's screen. Note that you can't view multiple windows side by side in the way you can on a PC.

● **Close a window**: To close a window, tap the round X button in its top left corner.

● **Open a new blank window**: Tap the blank space labelled New Page to start in a new empty window.

The multiple windows feature in Safari can be extremely useful, but you need to take care with it. If you use all nine windows and then tap a link that opens in a new window, you'll lose the contents of one of your previous windows. That doesn't matter so much if you were just reading a website, but if you had started to write something in Facebook or were midway through ordering a new fridge freezer, it might be annoying.

If a page is taking a long time to download, you can try reading another page in a different window while you wait.

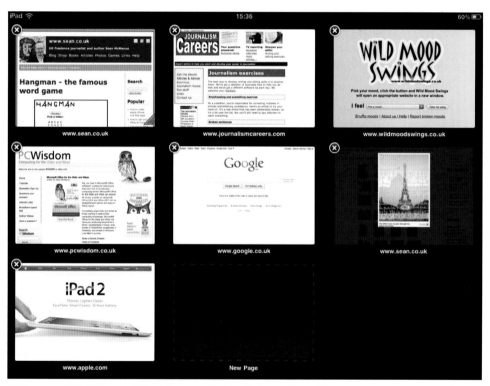

PC Wisdom is ©2000-2011 by John Wiley & Sons, Inc. Wild Mood Swings is ©1998-2011 Sean McManus. Google screenshot courtesy of Google.

Figure 7.6

Managing bookmarks, history and web clips

If you find a website you want to remember, you can bookmark it. This stores a link to the website in your browser so you can easily find it again.

The idea of bookmarking websites isn't limited to the iPad, and you've probably come across it on your computer. If so, you can synchronise your computer's bookmarks with your iPad. That will copy all your existing bookmarks from your computer to your iPad, and will copy any new bookmarks from your iPad back to your computer, too. Whenever you connect your iPad to your computer, your bookmarks will be updated on both devices.

To synchronise your bookmarks with your computer, follow these steps, referring to Figure 7.7:

1. Connect your iPad to your computer (see Chapter 2).

2. In iTunes on your computer, click the name of your iPad on the left.

3. Click to go into the Info category.

4. Scroll down to the Other section and tick the box to Sync bookmarks with your browser. If you have more than one browser installed on your computer, choose the one you use for your bookmarks from the menu.

5. Click Apply in the bottom right, then wait for iTunes to finish synchronising.

6. After iTunes has finished synchronising, eject your iPad.

Visiting websites using bookmarks

Your iPad comes with a handful of bookmarks on it already, including one that takes you to the iPad User Guide. There are two ways you can visit a website that's in your bookmarks.

The first is to use the address field. As you type into it, your browser will check your bookmarks to see if any of them match what you're typing. If they do, it will suggest those websites, so that you can just tap the website's name to visit it. This happens automatically whenever you're using the address field. Start typing 'bbc. co.uk', for example, and you'll see any pages on the BBC site you've bookmarked, which could be the news section or sites dedicated to your favourite shows.

Step 3

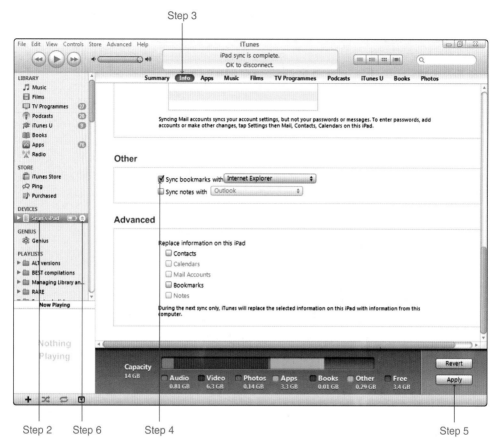

Step 2   Step 6   Step 4   Step 5

Figure 7.7

You don't have to type an address into the address field to find a bookmark; you can also type words that are in your bookmark title. Try typing 'user' into the address field, and you'll see the iPad User Guide link appears, even though its actual address doesn't include the word 'user'.

The other way you can visit websites you have bookmarked is to browse your bookmarks. If you don't have a particular website in mind and just fancy meandering through some of your favourite websites, this is the best approach.

To open your bookmarks, tap the Bookmarks button, which has an icon like a book (indicated in Figure 7.8). A menu will open, showing your bookmarks, including any you imported from your desktop computer. Each bookmark has a book icon beside it (see Figure 7.8) and you can tap the name or the icon to visit the website.

If you have lots of bookmarks, you can scroll the menu by dragging it.

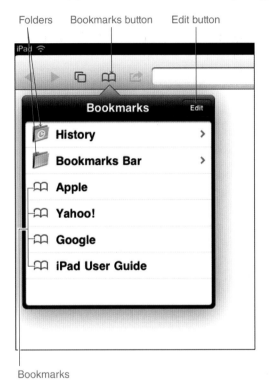

Figure 7.8

Organising your bookmarks in folders

Are you one of those people who spends more on stationery than on bread, or are you happy to throw your paperwork into a big box and hope you never need to find a gas bill at the bottom of it? Well, if you're an organised type, you'll be pleased to know you can arrange your browser bookmarks in folders. If you're not, feel free to skip this bit. You can always jump straight to a bookmark by typing in part of its name or address in Safari's address field. Organised bookmarks are much easier to browse, though.

> If you synchronise with the bookmarks on your computer, they'll arrive on your iPad in the folders they were in on your computer.

As you can see in Figure 7.8, Safari already has two folders set up on it:

● **History**: This stores links to the websites you've visited recently. You can't add your own bookmarks to this folder, but you can tap the History folder and then tap Clear History to delete this record. As you saw at the start of this chapter, the history is used to suggest websites when you're typing into the address field, so it makes it easier to visit sites you've been to before.

● **Bookmarks Bar**: The bookmarks bar appears underneath the address field when you're using it (see Figure 7.1 at the start of this chapter). This is a good place to keep your favourite websites. To visit one of them, tap the address field to make the bookmarks bar appear, and then tap the name of the website. Your bookmarks bar will be empty at first, but I'll show you how to add websites to it shortly.

You need to create a folder before you can add a bookmark to it. To create additional folders, tap the Edit button (shown in Figure 7.8). A new menu then appears, with a New Folder option in the top-left (shown in Figure 7.9). When you tap that, you're asked to enter a title for the new folder. There's only room for a few words here, so keep it short and put the important words at the start.

It's possible to have folders inside folders, so underneath the folder title, the iPad shows you which folder your new folder will appear in. Usually this just says Bookmarks, which means you'll see your folder as soon as you open your bookmarks. You can leave this setting alone, but if you tap it, you can pick one of your other folders to put this new folder inside.

When you've finished setting up your new folder, tap the Bookmarks button in the top left of the menu, or tap Done on the keyboard.

New folder

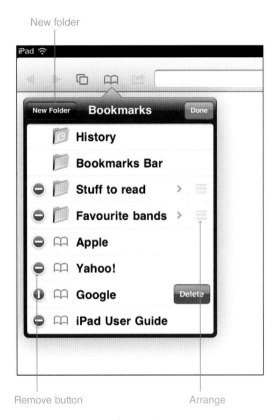

Remove button   Arrange

Figure 7.9

When you're in the edit mode, you can change the order of your folders. Put your finger on the Arrange icon (three short lines) to the right of the folder name and without removing your finger, move it up or down the list to change where that folder appears. The folder will stay where your finger is when you lift it from the iPad. This same technique can be used to rearrange the order of your bookmarks, but you can't change the order of Apple's default bookmarks and folders.

Deleting bookmarks

You can also delete bookmarks or folders, except for the History and Bookmarks Bar folders. When you edit a folder of bookmarks, red buttons will appear beside those items you can remove, shown in Figure 7.9. Tap one of these buttons, and a red button marked 'Delete' appears to the right of the item. Tap the Delete button to confirm, and your folder or bookmark is gone.

You can also swipe your finger left or right across a bookmark to make a Delete button appear. You don't have to tap the Edit button first if you do that.

When you're creating or deleting folders or bookmarks, don't tap the Edit button until you're looking at the folder or bookmarks you want to change. If you want to delete a bookmark that's in another folder, for example, tap that folder name first to show the bookmark, and then tap Edit so you can delete it.

Adding bookmarks

Now that you've set up the folders for your bookmarks, you can start to add bookmarks to them. The first step in adding a bookmark is to visit the website you'd like to add in the usual way.

To bookmark the web page you're viewing, tap the Bookmark/Share button – the icon that shows an arrow coming out of a box, indicated in Figure 7.10. When you tap it, a menu opens showing several options, two of which are:

- **Add to Home Screen**: If you tap this, the website you're viewing will be given an icon on your Home screen, like an app. This is called a web clip. You'll be prompted to enter a name to go underneath the icon, but you only have about 10–15 characters, depending on how wide they are, otherwise your iPad will abbreviate the name to the first few and last few letters. Some websites provide icons designed especially for web clips, but the iPad will use a tiny picture of the website if no icon is provided. When you tap the icon on the Home screen, Safari will open and take you straight to that website. I recommend you add your favourite websites to the Home screen so you can go straight to them. In Chapter 12, you'll learn how to organise and delete icons on your Home screen, including web clips.

- **Add Bookmark**: Tap this to add a bookmark, using the options shown in Figure 7.10. The name of the bookmark will be taken from the title of the web page, and some will make more sense than others. You can change the bookmark name to be anything you like, and you aren't limited to a short length restriction like you are with web clips. You can use the editing controls you've seen in the Mail and Notes apps: tap and hold to make the magnifying glass appear so you can reposition the insertion point for editing; and tap the X button in the title box to clear it. Underneath the bookmark name, you can see the folder it will appear in, which is usually Bookmarks. That means it will go into your bookmarks collection without being filed in a folder. If you want to put the bookmark in a folder you've created, tap the folder name and then choose which folder you want to put your new bookmark in. You can also add the bookmark to the Bookmarks bar. When you've finished, tap Save.

PC Wisdom is Copyright ©2000-2011 by John Wiley & Sons, Inc.

Figure 7.10

Whatever you type in the bookmark's title can be used to find it in the address bar. So feel free to add any words to the end of your bookmark titles that might make the bookmarks easier to find later.

Sharing website content

The web is all about sharing information, and you'll often come across information or pictures online that you want your friends to enjoy too. Safari has several features that make it easy to share website content.

Firstly, you can copy text or a mixture of text and images from a web page using one of the techniques you use in Notes or Mail. Tap and hold your finger on text near the content you want to copy, and the magnifying glass will appear. When you lift your finger, you can select the area you want to copy by moving the grab points, as you learned in Chapter 3. When you tap Copy, the text, images and their layout will be kept in the iPad's memory. You can then go into your Mail app, or other compatible apps, and use Paste to put the content into a new message or other document. For this technique to work, it's important that you tap and hold on ordinary text, and not on a link or image, otherwise a menu will appear instead of the magnifying glass.

Sometimes you can select a whole section of a web page by tapping and holding at the top of that section.

If you only want to copy a picture, tap and hold it. You'll be given the option to copy the picture so that you can paste it into an email or other document, or save it. If you save the picture, it will be stored with all your other photos on your iPad. In Chapter 11, you'll learn how to use the Photos app to view the pictures on your iPad.

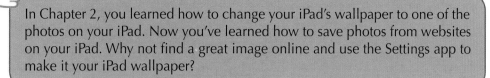

In Chapter 2, you learned how to change your iPad's wallpaper to one of the photos on your iPad. Now you've learned how to save photos from websites on your iPad. Why not find a great image online and use the Settings app to make it your iPad wallpaper?

There are two further options when you tap the Bookmark/Share icon in Safari:

- **Mail Link to this Page**: Tap this and the Mail app will open, with a new email already started. In the body of the email will be a link to the current web page. Sending a link has the advantage that whoever you're mailing can go straight to the website you want them to see, but it might not mean much to them without some context so it's worth writing a few words to explain what's on the website and why you're sending it to them. You can then go back to the Safari browser to carry on where you left off.

- **Print**: If you have an iPad-compatible printer, you can tap this to print the page. This option feels like the odd one out in this menu to me, because the others are all about keeping and sharing links to the web page. But if you imagine you're printing it for a friend, it's easy to remember where to find the Print button.

Summary

- Your iPad's web browser app is called Safari.

- When you are entering a website address, a .com key appears on the keyboard to help you.

- Tap and hold the .com key to use other extensions, including .co.uk.

- Tap and hold in the address field or in a text entry box to reposition the insertion point, copy or paste.

- Your browser keeps a record of the sites you visit to speed up return visits, but you can delete this record if you like.

- To zoom, double-tap a column or use the pinch gesture.

- You can drag or flick the page to scroll through it.

- To visit a link, tap it. To open it in a new window, tap and hold it.

- You can have up to nine web pages open at once.

- You can bookmark websites you want to revisit, or add a web clip, which puts an icon for the website on your Home screen.

- To find a bookmark, you can type part of its title into the address field.

- You can organise your bookmarks in folders.

- Bookmarks in the Bookmarks Bar folder are shown when you tap the address field.

- To copy text or a mixture of text and pictures, tap and hold on some text. To copy just a picture, tap and hold the picture.

- To save a picture, tap and hold the picture. It will be saved with all the other photos on your iPad.

Brain training

How will you fare in the traditional end of chapter quiz?

1. **To put a link to your favourite website on your Home screen, you:**
   (a) Add a bookmark to the Bookmarks Bar
   (b) Create a web clip
   (c) Add a bookmark to the website
   (d) Tap and hold the address bar

2. **If you mistype your email address into a text entry box on a website, you can reposition the insertion point by:**
   (a) Tapping the Delete key
   (b) Tapping and holding on the text entry box
   (c) Tapping the Go key
   (d) Tapping the Forward button

3. **When you finish typing information into one box on a form and want to go to the next, you should:**
   (a) Tap the Go key on the keyboard
   (b) Tap the Return key on the keyboard
   (c) Tap the next form box on the web page
   (d) Drag the web page

4. **To open a link in a new window, you can:**
   (a) Tap the link
   (b) Tap the Multiple Windows icon
   (c) Tap and hold a link
   (d) Double-tap a link

5. **To enlarge the website content, you can:**
   (a) Put two fingers on the iPad and move them closer together
   (b) Put two fingers on the iPad and move them further apart
   (c) Double-tap a column of text
   (d) Put your finger on the page and move it up the screen

Answers

Q1 – b   **Q2** – b. Deleting does reposition the insertion point but you have to retype text you've typed correctly since the mistake.   **Q3** – c   **Q4** – b and c   **Q5** – b and c

Visiting friends using Maps

8

Equipment needed: An iPad with an Internet connection (Wi-Fi or 3G).

Skills needed: Experience of starting apps (see Chapter 2), using the keyboard (see Chapter 3), managing bookmarks (see Chapter 7) and using the Contacts app (see Chapter 4).

If you get lost, your trusty iPad can show you the way. It uses information about the Wi-Fi network or cellular network you're using, plus satellite positioning technology if you have a 3G iPad, to work out where you are.

If you have disabled the location services in the Settings app to preserve battery life, you'll need to enable them again to use the Maps app.

The Maps app enables you to view street maps, satellite photos, photos of buildings, and traffic jams. It's powered by Google Maps, so if you've used that website it will be familiar to you. The Maps app uses many ideas you've come across in previous chapters, including bookmarks and the pinch gesture (see Chapter 7) and contacts (see Chapter 4).

In this chapter, I'll show you to how to use the app to plot a trip to visit a friend. First, tap the Maps icon on your Home screen or use the Spotlight search to start the app.

To use the Maps app, you need to have an Internet connection.

Finding where you are on the map

When the Maps app opens, it shows you where it thinks you are, using a blue pin. Around it is a blue ring that tells you how confident the iPad is in its guess: the larger the ring, the less precise the position is. Usually, it's accurate enough for you to find your way around easily.

To get an idea of the surrounding area, you can use a couple of gestures you've seen in other apps. You can drag the map around by putting your finger on it and moving it. New bits of the map are downloaded from the Internet as they're needed, so it might take a moment for the new map information to appear. At any time, you can jump back to your current location on the map by tapping the arrow icon, indicated in Figure 8.1.

You can use the pinch gesture you learned in Chapter 7 to zoom in and out, too. You can even zoom all the way out to see where you are on a global map. Suddenly, the world doesn't seem so small after all.

A double-tap will zoom in, and you can double-tap repeatedly to keep enlarging the map until you can't zoom any further. Use the finger pinch to zoom out again.

This app offers four different types of map: Classic (a streetmap), Satellite (which shows satellite photographs), Hybrid (which shows satellite photos with roads overlaid on top) and Terrain (which uses colour to indicate the height of the land). To change between them, tap in the bottom right of the screen to 'peel back' the map to reveal the options (see Figure 8.2). You can also switch on the Traffic option, which colour codes some roads to show you whether the traffic is currently flowing (green), slow (yellow) or jammed (red).

Arrow   Search box

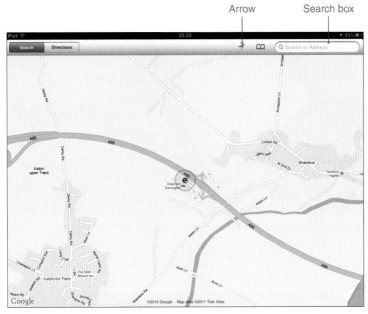

©2010 Google. Map data ©2011 Tele Atlas

Figure 8.1

The iPad enables you to drop a pin on the map as a place marker. Just tap and hold on the map, and a purple pin will drop from the sky at that point. If you tap the Drop Pin button, which appears when you tap in the bottom right of the map, a pin is placed in the middle of the map. You can only have one dropped pin at a time, so it's better to create a bookmark for places you want to remember, as you'll discover later in this chapter. The iPad has a compass built in to it, too. Tap the Arrow icon so it shows your current location and is coloured blue, and then tap it again. To calibrate the compass, you might need to wave the iPad around in the air in a figure of eight pattern (seriously – I'm not making this up!). You'll see instructions on screen if you need to do this. When the compass is active, a triangle shines out of the blue pin on the map, like the beam of headlights in a cartoon strip. It shows you the direction you're looking in, assuming you're holding the iPad in front of you. The Arrow icon changes its appearance when the compass is active. Just tap this again to turn the compass off.

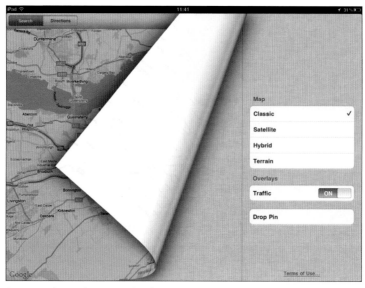

©2010 Google. Map data ©2011 Tele Atlas

Figure 8.2

See if you can find a satellite photo of your house, or wherever you are at the moment. Start by finding your current location, switch the view to satellite, and then zoom in.

Getting directions to a friend's house

You can find any place in the world by typing a place name into the Search box in the top right of the screen. Try 'Eiffel Tower' and 'Downing Street', for example. If you enter a street name with more than one match, the app will ask you which one you want before displaying it.

You can also use the addresses in the Contacts app. Here's how you get directions to a friend's house:

1. Tap the Bookmarks icon. This looks the same as it does in Safari and is indicated in Figure 8.3.

Bookmarks

Street view   Information   Contacts

©2010 Google. Map data ©2011 Tele Atlas

Figure 8.3

2. A menu will open (see Figure 8.3). If your contacts aren't showing, tap Contacts in the bottom right of the menu.

3. Use the Search box at the top of the menu, or scroll the alphabetically sorted list to find your friend and then tap his or her name.

4. The map moves to your friend's house and a red pin is dropped with their name above it, as you can see for Humphrey Appleby in Figure 8.3.

Once you've found your friend's house, you can zoom in in the usual way. If there's an icon of a person next to their name above their pin, then you can tap it to see a street view of their road, which will look similar to the one in Figure 8.4. This shows you panoramic photos that have been taken of the street by one of Google's roving cars, tricycles or (more rarely) snowmobiles. Street names appear down the middle of the roads, and you can tap the arrows on them to move along the street. Tap on the photo and move your finger around to spin the view through 360 degrees or look up and down. This is a great way to check for landmarks on the route before you leave, which can help you get your bearings when you get there. If your friend says you need to take the lane after the post office, for example, you can do a recce on the iPad first and more easily recognise it while you're driving along at 30mph. When you've finished, tap the circle with the map in it at the bottom right to go back to the map.

©Google.

Figure 8.4

If you tap the information icon on the label on someone's pin, it will show you their address and allow you to choose whether you want directions to their house or from their house. If you tap for directions to their house, a blue line is drawn on the map to show the route you need to take. At the bottom of the screen, a blue bar appears. It has three icons for travelling by car, by public transport and on foot. Tap your preferred mode of transport, and you'll see the estimated travel time. Tap the Start button in the blue bar to begin your directions.

If you're using public transport, tap the clock icon in the blue bar (where available) to see the timetable.

You can advance through the directions in the blue bar one at a time by tapping the Next and Previous buttons shown in Figure 8.5. You can also tap the List button (shown in Figure 8.5) to see all your instructions in a list, as in Figure 8.6. You can scroll this list and tap the steps in it to see them illustrated on the map. To hide the list again, tap the button indicated in Figure 8.6.

List   Previous direction

                                                    Next direction

Figure 8.5

Hopefully, that will help your visit go smoothly! If you fancy an excursion with the friends you're visiting or you want to plan other routes, you can get directions between any two places. Tap Directions in the top left first, if necessary, and then enter the start and end places in the boxes in the top right (see Figure 8.6). The button between the two boxes is used to reverse them, so that you can see directions for your return trip.

If there's a place you want to remember, tap and hold your finger on the map and a pin will drop there. Like the pins your contacts have, this has an Information button you can use for plotting routes, and a Street View button. You can only have one dropped pin at a time, so if you want to keep a record of an address, you need to create a bookmark for it. Tap the pin's Information button and then tap Add to Bookmarks. You enter a name for the bookmark, and then tap Save. You can see your bookmarks by tapping the Bookmarks button (see Figure 8.3) and then tapping Bookmarks in the bottom left of the menu that opens.

When you've finished with your directions, you can bring back the Search box again by tapping Search in the top left (see Figure 8.6). If your journey has worked up a thirst, try searching for café (or pub!) to see all the refreshment stops on the map.

The Bookmarks menu can also show you Recents, the places and directions you last searched for and the location of your current dropped pin.

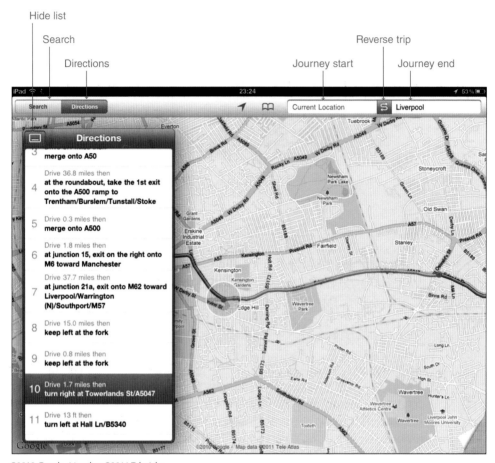

Hide list

Search

Directions

Reverse trip

Journey start

Journey end

Directions

3   merge onto A50

Drive 36.8 miles then
4   at the roundabout, take the 1st exit
     onto the A500 ramp to
     Trentham/Burslem/Tunstall/Stoke

Drive 0.3 miles then
5   merge onto A500

Drive 1.8 miles then
6   at junction 15, exit on the right onto
     M6 toward Manchester

Drive 37.7 miles then
7   at junction 21a, exit onto M62 toward
     Liverpool/Warrington
     (N)/Southport/M57

Drive 15.0 miles then
8   keep left at the fork

Drive 0.8 miles then
9   keep left at the fork

10   Drive 1.7 miles then
     turn right at Towerlands St/A5047

11   Drive 13 ft then
     turn left at Hall Ln/B5340

©2010 Google. Map data ©2011 Tele Atlas

Figure 8.6

Using Maps to update your address book

The Maps app can help you to keep your address book updated, and sometimes it's quicker to find an address in Maps than to type it in – especially if you're already there.

Here's how. When you're at a friend's house, connect using 3G or ask your friend if you can use their Wi-Fi. In the Maps app, tap the arrow to find your current location, tap the blue pin, tap the Information button in the label that opens and then choose Add to Contacts. You can then add the address of where you are to an existing or new contact. Don't forget to edit the house number and post code to make sure they're accurate, using the techniques you learned in Chapter 3.

You can also add addresses using dropped pins, from the comfort of your home. Find an address on the map, tap and hold, and then tap the Information button on the label that opens. The iPad will invite you to add that address to a new or existing contact.

Summary

- To use Maps on your iPad, you need to have an Internet connection and location services enabled.

- Tap the Arrow icon to see your current location. Tap it again to turn the compass on.

- The blue pin shows you where you are on the map.

- You can drag the map and double-tap or pinch to zoom.

- To choose the map type and turn on traffic settings, tap in the bottom right of the map.

- Use the Search box to search for a place by name or a type of business.

- Tap and hold on the map to drop a pin.

- Tap the Bookmarks button to find your bookmarks and contacts on the map.

- Tap the Information button on a pin's label to plot a route to or from there, create a bookmark or add an address to a contact.

Brain training

Find out if you've mastered Maps with this short quiz.

1. Using the Maps app, you might be able to see:

(a) A friend's house, as seen from a taxi

(b) Your house, as viewed from space

(c) The Houses of Parliament, as seen from inside

(d) The terrain of the Alps

2. A yellow line along a road on the map means:

(a) It's a dirt track

(b) The road is closed

(c) Traffic is moving slowly

(d) There's been a custard spillage following a lorry accident

3. To see what a shop's front door looks like:

(a) Drop a pin and tap the Information button on its label

(b) Drop a pin and tap the person icon on its label

(c) Use the pinch gesture to zoom in

(d) Change the map view to Satellite

4. If you tap and hold a spot on the map, you can:

(a) Zoom in

(b) Zoom out

(c) Drop a pin

(d) See the street view at that spot

5. To go back to some directions you recently searched for:

(a) Tap the Previous button

(b) Tap the Bookmarks button

(c) Tap Directions

(d) Tap Reverse Trip

Answers

Q1 – a, b and d **Q2** – c **Q3** – b **Q4** – c and d **Q5** – b

PART III
Sound and Vision

I've downloaded our entire music collection from iTunes. Now nobody will be able to see what appalling taste we have.

Adding music and video to your iPad

9

Equipment needed: An iPad with an Internet connection. Your credit card, if you plan to download from the iTunes store. A computer with a CD drive and an Internet connection, if you want to copy CDs.

Skills needed: Experience using apps and gestures. Skills using the web browser (see Chapter 7) are particularly valuable.

One of Apple's shrewdest moves was to create the iTunes store, which sells audio and video content, and makes certain programmes available for free download. The iTunes store was launched in 2003 for iPod music players, and has made Apple one of the most powerful companies in the entertainment business. What it means for you is that you can find Hollywood blockbusters, TV shows, recent or classic albums and educational content, from the comfort of your sofa.

The content you choose (the programmes, films, and music) is copied straight into your iPad from the Internet, through a process called 'downloading'. Once your music or programmes have been downloaded, they're kept in the iPad so you can play them without needing an Internet connection in future. The process of downloading is fast and convenient. For example, you can discover a new album, hear some samples, buy your favourite songs, download them and start listening to them, all within a few minutes.

There's a fantastic catalogue on offer, including many classic films, TV series and songs that you might have thought you'd never experience again. I've particularly enjoyed watching vintage episodes of Dr Who and downloading rare songs by some of my favourite bands. There's a wealth of music there, from top acts of the 1950s and 1960s to today's chart-toppers. If you've got a favourite record you've lost, or a golden oldie you'd like to hear again, the iTunes store can help.

There is some potential for confusion here: Apple uses the name 'iTunes' to refer both to the software you run on your computer to manage your iPad, and to the store where you buy content for it.

In this chapter, I'll show you how you can use the iTunes store to download audio and video content for your iPad. Even if you don't want to buy music or films, it's worth investigating the iTunes store. As I'll show you, there's lots of free content there too.

What about your CD collection? The good news is that you can use the iTunes software on your computer to copy your music CDs to your iPad. I'll show you how to do that too, so that you'll be ready to explore how to play music and video on your iPad in Chapter 10.

Over 10 billion songs have been downloaded from the iTunes store since it launched. The 10 billionth was *Guess Things Happen That Way* by Johnny Cash, downloaded on 24 February 2010. Coincidentally, that was also the 55th birthday of Steve Jobs, Apple's well-known Chief Executive Officer.

Browsing the iTunes store

To get started, tap the iTunes icon on your iPad's Home screen. This is short for 'iTunes store', so when it opens, you'll see something that looks a bit like a shopping website. Figure 9.1 shows you what the store's home page looks like.

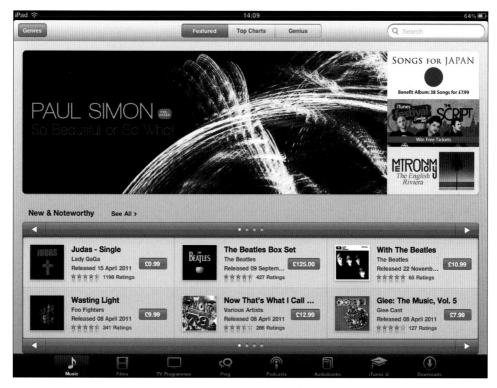

Figure 9.1

You navigate the store similar to the way you use a website (see Chapter 7). You can drag the page up to see content that doesn't fit on the screen, and then tap the status bar to jump back to the top of the page. When you see a product or promotion you want to find out more about, tap it to open it the way you do with a link on a web page. At the bottom of the scrolling page, there are buttons to manage your account, redeem gift vouchers or seek support. Across the top of the screen are buttons to select different genres (such as rock, pop or comedy) and to see the bestselling content (tap Top Charts).

Along the bottom of the screen, at all times, is a series of buttons that you use to navigate the different types of content in the store. The menu has options for:

● **Music,** which includes music videos. Free downloads are made available from time to time, including a free single of the week. But you'll have to pay for nearly all the content in this section.

- **Films.** You can buy a film, or rent it, which costs less. Buying a film means you can watch it as often as you like, for as long as you like. Rented films expire 48 hours after you start watching them (24 hours in the US), and will then automatically be deleted from your iPad. If you don't get around to watching a film you've rented, it'll be deleted after 30 days anyway.

- **TV Programmes**, including US and UK drama, comedy and children's shows. As with music, there are occasional free downloads, but nearly all the content is for sale.

- **Ping**. This is a place where you can tell other people who use it what you think about certain artists.

- **Podcasts**, which are regular programmes you can download for free. Many radio broadcasters make edited versions of their shows available for free download, for example, but anyone can create a podcast, so there's a lot of material independently published, too. Podcasts can use video or be audio-only. A good place to start is by searching for BBC to find podcasts of Desert Island Discs, Radio 4's Friday Night Comedy, 5 Live Football Daily, The Archers, and many more radio programmes from across the BBC's stations.

- **Audiobooks**, which are professionally recorded readings of books, and radio programmes. You have to pay for these.

- **iTunes U**, where the U is short for University. No sitting at the back giggling here: you've got a front row seat at some of the world's leading institutions, including Oxford and Cambridge universities, both of which provide recordings of their lectures for free download.

- **Downloads**, which shows you the progress of content you're downloading to your iPad.

To search the store, tap the search box in the top right of the screen. It doesn't matter what part of the store you're in when you do this because it will show you results from across the store.

> If you're learning a language, you can often download podcasts of radio programmes in that language, especially the news.

Buying music and video from iTunes

We've all bought an album in a shop and felt cheated when we got it home because it only had two good songs on it. On the iTunes Store, there's much less risk of this because it allows you to preview the music tracks first, to make sure you like them. You can usually buy individual songs without having to buy the whole album, too. Buying one song is cheaper, but a whole album is often better value than cherry-picking several songs.

Once you've found an album you'd like to buy (by browsing the featured products or using the search), tap its artwork to see the tracks on it. A new window opens in the middle of the screen, as you can see in Figure 9.2. You can drag this window up and down to see more information, including reviews by other customers where available.

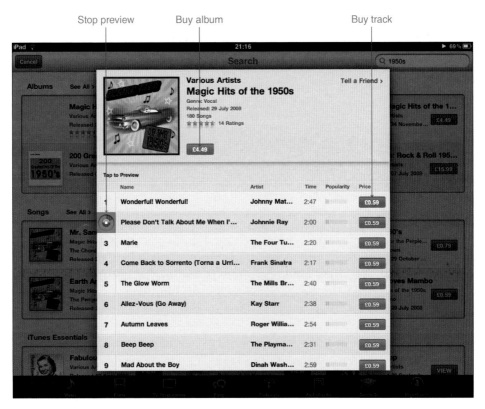

Figure 9.2

To hear a sample of a track, tap its name. You can stop the song playing again by tapping the Stop button that appears in place of its track number. If you don't hear anything, check you have your iPad's volume switched on. To close the album's window and carry on browsing the store, tap outside the album window.

When you've found something you want to buy, tap the price beside the track name; or, to buy the whole album, tap the price underneath the album name at the top (both indicated in Figure 9.2). The Price button will change to a Buy Song or Buy Album button. Tap that, and you'll be prompted to log in to your iTunes account. This is the same account you created when you set up your iPad (see Chapter 2). Usually, your credit card will then be charged and your content will be downloaded.

The first time you buy something, though, you will also be required to confirm your payment information. You'll be shown your account information, and will need to tap beside where it says 'security code' and enter the three-digit security number on the back of your credit card. When you've finished confirming your details, tap Done in the top right of the window. You'll get a last chance to back out, but once you tap Buy, your credit card will be charged and your music will start to download – so make sure you're certain you want to buy it before you tap Buy.

Tap Artist Page, in the top right of an album's window, to quickly find other albums by the same artist.

Once you've mastered downloading music, the process for downloading TV shows and films is similar. You can search for a particular programme, or browse through the featured titles. When you find something you like, tap its artwork to open its window. The main difference here is that for TV episodes you tap the picture from the episode to see the preview and for films you tap the Preview button on the right.

For video content, you might also be offered two different formats: HD and standard (SD). HD is short for high definition and is a higher quality video format. It looks much sharper on the iPad's screen, but standard definition is acceptable and is the only format available for older TV shows.

Films are sometimes released in different definitions at different times. At the time of writing, one of the Harry Potter films can be bought or rented in standard definition, but the HD version is only available to rent.

To download free content, including podcast episodes and iTunes U programmes, tap the Free button that appears in place of a price.

Content is queued up and downloaded one item at a time. It can take several minutes for a film to download, but you can use other apps on your iPad while the downloading continues in the background. To check the progress of your downloads, tap the Downloads button at the bottom of the screen in the iTunes app.

The process of buying is quick and convenient, so much so that you can forget you're spending money. It feels very different to handing over £10 notes in a record shop, so keep an eye on how much you're spending in the iTunes store.

For advice on playing music and video on your iPad, see Chapter 10.

Using the iTunes store on your computer

If you prefer, you can download content from the iTunes store on your computer. Open the iTunes software on your computer and click iTunes Store on the left. Across the top of the screen are buttons that take you to the different types of content (such as music, films and TV).

There are a few additional features in the iTunes store on your computer. One is that you can add content to a wishlist by clicking the arrow button beside its price. You can view all the items on your wishlist by clicking the arrow beside your email address in the top right.

Another useful addition is that you can subscribe to podcasts, so that your computer automatically downloads the latest episode when you open iTunes. When you view a podcast's details in the iTunes store on your computer, you can click the Free button beside an episode to download just that episode, or click the Subscribe button underneath its artwork to subscribe for free.

When you synchronise your iPad with your computer, any content you down-loaded on your computer can be copied to your iPad.

Backing up your content and synchronising with your computer

When you connect your iPad to your computer, any content you bought on your iPad is automatically copied to your computer. This means you have a 'backup' of your content saved on your computer. You can check content has copied across to your computer by going into the iTunes software on your computer, clicking the content type (such as 'TV Programmes') on the left and using the search box if necessary in the top right to find that particular item.

You can set your iPad to automatically copy all the new content you download on your computer to your iPad, too, but there is a drawback with this; if you keep adding content to your iPad it could eventually get full up, especially if you're a movie buff. The synchronisation options in iTunes enable you to choose what gets copied from your computer to your iPad. Since there's a backup copy of every-thing on your computer, you can also use the synchronisation options to tempo-rarily remove content from the iPad that you might want to put back on again later.

Figure 9.3 shows the synchronisation options for TV programmes. On the left, you can see the different TV programmes I've bought. On the right, you can see the specific episodes. The blue spot beside an episode means you haven't watched it yet, and a half-filled spot means you've only watched part of it. You can tick any episodes or series you'd like to copy to your iPad. If there are any on your iPad that you don't need there any more, you can untick them to remove them from the iPad but keep them on your computer.

At the top of the screen, there are options for automatically copying all pro-grammes or episodes of specific programmes from your computer to your iPad, based on whether you've watched them and how new they are. There are similar options for choosing the films, podcasts and music (by artist, genre and playlist) you want to be copied onto your iPad.

Figure 9.3

A playlist is a list of songs or videos (see Chapter 10) that can be played in order. Content you buy on your iPad is also added to a playlist on your computer, called Purchased on Your iPad (where 'Your iPad' is the name you gave your iPad when you set it up). In the iTunes software on your computer, you can find this playlist on the left sidebar (see Figure 9.3), and this is another handy way to check content has been copied from your iPad to your computer.

Click the content categories (Music, Films, TV Programmes, Podcasts, iTunes U) at the top of the screen in the iTunes software on your computer to see the different options, and click Apply when you've finished making your selections.

Adding CDs to your iPad using your computer

Of course, most of us have already paid good money to own the music we love, so we'd rather not buy it again. The good news is that you can transfer CDs to your iPad, as long as your computer has a CD drive. Under copyright law, you are only allowed to copy CDs with the permission of whoever created them. However, a lot of people consider it ethical to copy CDs they've bought themselves to their own device for playing them, as long as they continue to own the original CDs. Copying CDs to your computer like this is called 'ripping' them. (It's considered unfair to the artists and companies who invest in them to copy CDs you haven't bought, or to pass your own copies around friends.)

Sometimes it's cheaper to buy a CD and rip it using your computer than it is to buy the same album as a download.

To add a CD to your iPad, follow these steps:

1. Start the iTunes software on your computer and insert your music CD in the CD drive.

2. iTunes will download the names of songs and artists from the Internet if possible, as shown in Figure 9.4. If this fails, or you need to correct a piece of information, right-click on a song and choose Get Info from the menu. Click the Info tab and you can then add or edit the song title, band name, genre and year. To change information that applies to all the tracks at the same time, use CTRL+A on the keyboard to select them all, then right-click on a track and choose Get Info.

3. Untick any songs you don't wish to copy.

4. Click Import CD in the bottom right. The CD drive will start to whirr, and your CD will be copied to your computer.

You can play any CDs you've copied to your computer, and any content you've downloaded from Apple's store, using the iTunes software on your computer as well as your iPad. Find the content you want to play by clicking the content type on the left (eg music), and then using the search box if necessary in the top right.

You can double-click a song name to start it playing, and there are CD-player-like controls in the top left to pause and jump forward or back a track.

You can't copy DVDs to your iPad using iTunes, unfortunately, because DVDs have encryption to stop them being copied. There is third-party software available online that you can use to copy DVDs into iTunes, but it's much more complex than using iTunes to copy CDs.

When you synchronise your iPad with your computer, any CDs you've added to your computer will be copied from your computer to your iPad in accordance with your synchronisation settings. If your CD doesn't get copied to your iPad, check that you have set your computer to synchronise either all music or that particular artist, album or genre.

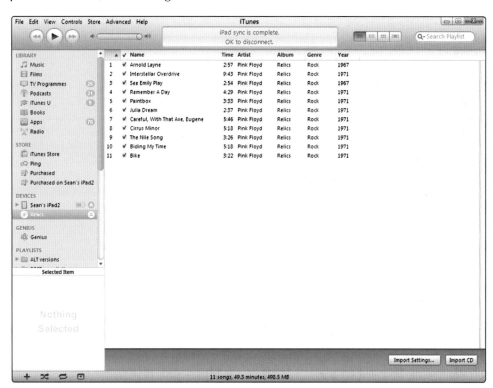

Figure 9.4

Now you've learned how to add music and video to your iPad, in the next chapter we'll look at how you can play it.

One popular way of storing music on a computer is in a file called an MP3, and your iPad can play any song in that format. You can buy MP3 music downloads from Amazon using your computer. When you search in Amazon for a particular album or artist, you will often be given the choice to download an MP3 album instead of buying a CD. Amazon provides some free software that will copy the MP3s you buy to your iTunes software for you automatically. You can't buy music downloads from Amazon on your iPad. Instead, shop on your computer, and your purchases can be copied to your iPad when you next synchronise your computer with your iPad. Amazon often has a different product range and pricing structure to the iTunes store, so it's worth shopping around.

Summary

- You can download music and video content from the iTunes store, either on your iPad or by using your computer.

- You have to pay for most content, but you can download podcasts and iTunes U courses for free.

- You navigate the store similar to the way you navigate a website.

- You can buy individual songs or TV episodes, or a whole album or TV series.

- For a brief sample before you buy on your iPad, tap the name of the music track, the picture of the TV show or the Film Preview button.

- High definition films and TV programmes are better quality, but older films and programmes are only available in standard definition.

- Any content you buy on your iPad is copied onto your computer when you synchronise with it, and is kept there as a 'back-up'.

- You can choose which TV shows, films, podcasts and music are put onto your iPad. They are all stored on your computer, including the ones that aren't on your iPad so you can still put them on your iPad later.

- You can copy your music CDs to your computer using the iTunes software on it. Then you can copy the music to your iPad from your computer when you synchronise your iPad with your computer.

Brain training

Hopefully, your iPad is now packed full of great videos and music you can enjoy. Use this quick quiz to check whether you've mastered the art of adding music and video to your iPad.

1. You can buy content for your iPad using:

(a) The iPod app on your iPad

(b) The iTunes app on your iPad

(c) The iTunes software on your computer

(d) The App Store app on your iPad

2. To be able to watch a Hollywood film on your iPad whenever you like and as often as you like, you can:

(a) Rip a DVD using iTunes

(b) Buy a film in the iTunes store

(c) Rent a film in the iTunes store

(d) Download in high definition

3. When you synchronise your iPad with your computer:

(a) Any content bought on your iPad is copied to your computer

(b) All the content on your computer is copied to your iPad

(c) The content you select is copied from your computer to your iPad

(d) You can choose to remove content from your iPad for now

4. If you tap the price beside a song in the iTunes app, it will:

(a) Start a preview of that song

(b) Start the buying process for that album

(c) Start the buying process for that song

(d) Download that album to your computer

5. If you tap the picture beside a TV episode in the iTunes app, it will:

(a) Enlarge the picture

(b) Show you the chapters in that episode

(c) Start the buying process for that episode

(d) Play a preview of the episode

Answers

Q1 – b and c   **Q2** – b   **Q3** – a, c and d   **Q4** – c   **Q5** – d

Playing audio and video on your iPad

10

Equipment needed: An iPad with audio and/or video content loaded onto it (see Chapter 9), and/or an Internet connection for watching YouTube videos. Earphones if you'd like to use them.

Skills needed: Good command of gestures, including tapping and dragging. Experience using Windows applications (clicking, scrolling, mouse control) if you want to make playlists on your computer.

The iPad enables you to take your favourite music and videos with you wherever you go, and gives you a number of interesting new ways to enjoy your music collection. If there is one track in the middle of your favourite album that really niggles you, or if you've always wanted a jukebox that plays your favourite songs in a random order, the playlists feature can help.

The iPad's high-quality screen is also ideal for watching films, whether these are full-length movies you've bought or rented, or short films published on the Internet.

In this chapter, I'll show you how to play music and video on your iPad. I'll assume you've successfully added music or video to your iPad, by downloading it from the iTunes store or by ripping music from your CDs. Both of these were covered in Chapter 9, so refer back there for a refresher if necessary. If you haven't added any videos to your iPad, you can still try watching videos with the YouTube app, as I'll show you. You'll also learn how to play podcasts, audiobooks and iTunes U courses.

Playing audio content on your iPad

Again, Apple confuses the process by using the same word to mean two different things: the app used to play music on your iPad is called iPod, which is also the name of Apple's music player devices. In this chapter, we only use it to refer to the app. You can find the iPod app on the dock at the bottom of your Home screen. Tap it to start.

You can choose whether you want to listen to your music using earphones (which you'll need to buy separately) or not. If you have earphones, plug them into the round hole on the back of your iPad. It's in the top left corner when the Home button is at the bottom.

Browsing and playing your music

The iPod app gives you several different ways to browse through your music collection. By default, you see your content sorted by Songs, but you can tap the buttons at the bottom of the screen (See Figure 10.1) to see your music organised by Artists, Albums, Genres or Composers. The Composers view is particularly useful if you're a classical music fan, but most rock and pop music fans will rarely stray from the Songs, Artists and Albums views.

Figure 10.1 shows my music collection sorted by song title. If you don't see something similar on your iPad, tap Music in the left column (if necessary) and then tap Songs at the bottom of the screen.

You can drag the song list up and down, or use the search in the top right to find a particular track, album or artist. When you've found something you want to play, just tap the song name and it will start to play. Your music will continue to play even if you put the iPad into sleep mode, or if you press the Home button and go into another app. If you want to stop it playing again, go back into the iPod app and tap the Pause/Play button (see Figure 10.1).

At the top of the screen are various playback controls, indicated in Figure 10.1. In the top left, there is a volume indicator and control. Drag the round circle left to turn the volume down, or right to turn it up. You can also use the physical volume switch on your iPad (see Chapter 2) to change the volume and move the indicator.

Volume indicator and control

Playhead   Pause/Play

Back

Forward

Figure 10.1

If you can't hear anything, always check the volume first. It's almost too obvious to say, but we've all spent time shaking and tuning radios that just needed their volume nudging up.

In the middle at the top, are playback controls that are similar to those you might have seen marked on a CD player. The central button is used to start or pause playing. Tap the button to the left of it (indicated as the Back button in Figure 10.1) once to restart playing the current track from the beginning, or twice to go to the previous track. The button to the right of the Pause/Play button (the Forward button in Figure 10.1) skips to the next track.

You can also tap and hold these two buttons to fast forward or rewind through a track, but it's easier to use the playhead control underneath, which shows the progress of the playback. You can drag this left or right to go to any position in the song. The bar it slides in is always the same length whether the song lasts for 3 minutes or 30 minutes, so nudging the playhead a centimetre along the bar could advance the song a few seconds or a minute or more depending on the song's length. Sliding it to midway along the bar will always be halfway through the song, though.

Have a go at playing a few tracks, just to familiarise yourself with how the iPod app works.

Tap the Artists button at the bottom to see your music alphabetically sorted by artist, with details of how many songs and albums you have by each artist. Because the iPad can't tell the difference between the name of a person and the name of a band, it doesn't sort artists by surname, as you might expect. Instead, it sorts everything from the first letter of the first word, which means Paul McCartney comes after Frank Zappa. This can throw you a bit at first, but it makes a lot more sense than hunting for Pink Floyd under F or having the Rolling Stones under S. An exception to this sorting method is that iTunes ignores the word 'The', so you will still find The Beatles under B. If you tap the name of an artist, you can see which of their tracks and albums you have on your iPad. Tap any one of these to play it.

The Albums view is the most attractive (see Figure 10.2), showing the artwork for all your albums arranged in rows. As with the Songs and Artists view, you can drag up and down to see more. When you tap an album, a window opens to show you the tracks on it, and you can tap a track name to start that song playing.

The different views aren't purely cosmetic: when one song finishes, they also decide what song will play next. If you choose the Songs view, the next song will be the next song alphabetically, no matter who the artist is. In the Artists view, it's the next song by the same artist. In the Albums view, it's the next song on the same album. If you have used the search box in the top right, the next song to play will be the next one in the list of search results.

Figure 10.2

Looping and shuffling your music

When a song is playing, there are two different ways the iPad will behave. It will either have the song's artwork filling its screen or show a small version of the artwork in the bottom left, so you can continue browsing your music on screen. When the artwork is in the corner, you can tap it to make it fill the screen, as in Figure 10.3.

When the artwork is filling the screen (the 'artwork view'), you can tap it to reveal the standard playback controls (shifted around slightly). The volume control is in the top left, with the playback controls in the top right. You will see that some new controls appear as well (indicated in Figure 10.3):

● **Looping**: Tap this once to replay the list of songs from the beginning when it reaches the end of the list. When you tap it, the icon will go blue. You can also ask it to repeat the current song by tapping it again; a 1 will appear on the icon, and the song currently playing will repeat. Tap it again to turn off looping.

● **Shuffle**: This plays the songs in a random order. Tap it once to activate it (the icon goes blue) and tap it again to turn it off.

- **Show songs on this album**: Tap the button in the bottom right to see all the songs on the same album as the song that's playing. In this view, you can also rate your music, giving it one to five stars by tapping one of the five dots underneath the playhead control.

- **Close artwork view**: Tap this to go back to the Songs, Artists, Albums, Genres or Composers view.

Album artwork © Tom Hingley

Figure 10.3

Creating a playlist on your iPad

One of the best features of digital music is that it allows you to create your own playlists, which enable you to cue up a list of songs you'd like to hear. You could create a playlist of background music for a party, a set of songs that put you in a good mood, or a list of your favourite tracks from a particular artist. The lists can be as short or long as you like, and you can put the songs in any order you like.

You can use shuffle to listen to a playlist, too, to mix up the order songs are played in and add an element of surprise.

To create a playlist on your iPad, follow these steps:

1. Tap the + button in the bottom left of the screen (the Create Playlist button, indicated in Figure 10.4).

Genius playlist

Create playlist

Album artwork © Nero Schwarz Ltd

Figure 10.4

2. Think of a name for your playlist, type it in, and tap Save. You'll often only see the first few words of a playlist's name onscreen, so make sure these are distinctive.

3. You'll see the list of all the songs on your iPad, but now you'll see there is a blue Add icon beside each song. To add a song to your playlist, tap its Add icon once. If you tap more than once, the song will be added to the list as many times as you tap it. You don't have to do this in Songs view – you can also choose songs by Artist, Album, Genre or Composer, by tapping the buttons at the bottom of the screen. (You can't use the search for this function, however.)

169

4. Once you've chosen all the songs you want to be in this particular playlist, tap Done in the top right. You'll see your playlist (see Figure 10.4), with a red Delete button beside each song. Tap this to remove any songs you don't want in your playlist any more. (Don't worry – this won't delete them from your iPad, only from this playlist.)

5. It's easy to change a song's place in the list: just tap and hold its three-bar icon on the right and move your finger up or down the screen. When you release your finger, the song will be dropped into that position in the playlist.

6. To add more songs, tap Add Songs in the top right. When you've finished, tap Done in the top right.

To go to your playlist, tap its name in the column on the left. You can then start playing from any track, or tap the Shuffle button at the top of the playlist to hear the songs in a random order. If you want to add more songs or take some out, go to your playlist and then tap Edit in the top right.

The iPad also has a feature called Genius, which is another way you can create playlists. If you first choose a song you like, then tap the Genius Playlist button, it will automatically generate a playlist of other songs that should sound good with your chosen song. To use Genius, you first need to enable it in iTunes on your computer (click Genius on the left and then click Turn on Genius). Once it's enabled, this will periodically send information about your music collection to Apple, which Apple analyses to create automatic playlists for you but may also use to recommend products to you. After turning on Genius on your computer, you need to synchronise your iPad with your computer so you can use Genius on your iPad.

Creating playlists using iTunes

You can also use the iTunes software on your computer to create playlists, and then use these playlists to choose which songs are synchronised to your iPad. Follow these steps:

1. On your computer, go into the iTunes software. Click on the File menu in the top left, and choose New Playlist.

2. Your new playlist will appear on the left. Choose a name for it, type it in and press the Enter/Return key.

3. Click Music at the top of the left-hand column.

4. Find a song you would like to add to your playlist. You can use the scrollbar to scroll up and down the list, or use the search box in the top right to go straight to a particular song, album or artist.

5. Click the song and, keeping the mouse button held down, move the mouse pointer to the name of your new playlist in the left hand column. Release your mouse button, and the song will be added to the playlist.

6. To see what's on the playlist, click its name in the left column. To change the order of songs, click a song and hold the mouse button down. Move the mouse pointer to where you want the song to be, then release the mouse button. The song will now be in its new position.

On your computer, you can also create smart playlists, which use simple rules to generate a playlist. These are very useful and can save you a lot of time adding songs manually. You can come up with lots of creative ways to explore your music collection using the information iTunes knows about your music.

Say you wanted to create a playlist of all the rock & roll music released before 1960 that you have in your iTunes library. Here's how you would do that:

1. On your computer, go into iTunes. Click on the File menu in the top left, and choose New Smart Playlist.

2. A window opens, like that shown in Figure 10.5. Click on the first pulldown menu. This has a list of different bits of information that iTunes holds about each piece of music you have, such as the artist who made it (Artist, in the menu), the album it comes from (Album), the year the song was released (Year), and how many times you've played it (Plays). In our example, you need to choose Genre, which is the type of music it is.

3. Click on the second pulldown menu. This gives you options such as 'contains', 'is' (or 'is not'), 'is after', 'is before' or 'is in the last'. For our example, you would choose 'is'.

4. Enter what you'd like to match with in the third box, such as the name of an artist or a time period. For our example, you would type 'Rock & Roll'. If you read across the three boxes, you can see it says 'Genre is Rock & Roll' (see Figure 10.5), which perfectly describes the music you want in this playlist.

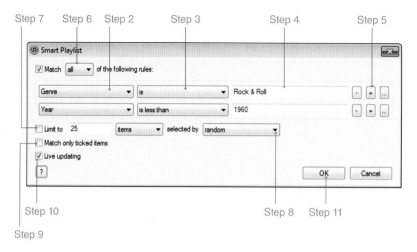

Figure 10.5

5. In our example, you also want to limit your choice to music that was released before 1960. You'll need to add another line of options to do that, so click on the + button at the end of the line you just completed to add another line. Repeat the process, this time choosing 'Year', 'is less than' and '1960'.

6. Now you have two rules for your playlist: songs that are rock & roll, and songs from before 1960. You can decide whether you want only songs that meet both these rules, or songs that meet either of the rules (which would include later rock & roll songs, and any other type of music from before 1960). For our example, we need all the rules to be applied, so choose All in the pulldown menu at the top.

7. There are three tickboxes at the bottom left. Tick the first of these if you'd like to limit the length of the playlist. You can choose to limit it by the number of songs on your playlist, the amount of time it takes to play the whole playlist or the total size of all the files in the playlist.

8. If you've limited the size of your playlist, choose how you want the songs to be chosen. They can be picked at random, or according to how often you've played them, how recently you added them to iTunes or long it is since you last played them.

9. If there are some songs that you don't want to go into this playlist, you can tick the box beside 'Match only ticked items'. Later, you can find the songs in

iTunes and untick the box beside their names to stop them being added to this playlist.

10. The playlists can update themselves, too. For example, say you have a playlist that includes all the music you've added to your library in the last month. As time goes by and you add more songs, that list will change. Every time you synchronise your iPad with your PC, that playlist will be updated with the music you added in the last month. To disable the updating of the playlist, untick the box beside 'Live updating'.

11. Click OK.

12. Your smart playlist appears on the left, but you'll see it has been given a name that has been generated automatically. Type a new name if you'd like to change it, and then press Enter.

It sounds more complicated than it is! The best way to get to grips with it is to try it out. Here are some ideas for how you can use this feature:

● To create a list of 25 random pop songs that you have added to your music library in the last six months, use: Genre is Pop; Date Added is in the last 6 months; Limit to 25 items selected by random.

● To fill 1GB of your iPad with your favourite rock songs, use: Genre contains Rock; Limit to 1GB selected by most often played.

● To make a playlist of Pink Floyd songs from the 1970s that you haven't yet played on your iPad or computer, use: Artist is Pink Floyd, Year is in the range 1970 to 1979; Plays is 0.

● To create a playlist of the latest 1GB of music added to your music library, use: Media Kind is Music; Limit to 1GB selected by most recently added.

You can synchronise multiple playlists with your iPad, so you might have a hand-picked playlist of your favourite songs, plus a smart playlist of new songs and maybe a smart playlist of random pop songs thrown in for good measure. That could give you just the right mix of music for your iPad, without you having to handpick every song.

To change a playlist name, double-click it. To delete a playlist, right-click on its name and then choose Delete.

Playing podcasts, audiobooks and iTunes U courses

You play podcasts, audiobooks and iTunes U programmes from the iPod app, too. On your iPad, go into the iPod app. Tap Podcasts on the left of the screen and you'll see all the different podcast series you've downloaded. You can tap one of these to find individual episodes within it, and then tap an episode to start it playing. If you choose a video podcast, it will open in the Videos app (see the following section). When it's finished, you can go back to your iPod app by pressing the Home button and then starting the iPod app again.

Your iTunes U courses and audiobooks are also found in the sidebar on the left. Tap the type of content you want, and you can then choose a specific lesson or audiobook to play.

Watching videos on your iPad

In Chapter 9, you learned how to add video content to your iPad, such as free lectures from some of the world's leading universities, vintage TV shows and Hollywood blockbusters. If you have an iPad with cameras, you'll also be able to shoot videos on it, as you'll see in Chapter 11.

There are three different apps that are used to play video on your iPad:

● **Videos**: This app is used to watch videos you've bought or downloaded from iTunes (see Chapter 9). If you try to play a music video or video podcast in the iPod app, the Videos app will open automatically to play that content.

● **YouTube**: This app enables you to watch short films from the video-sharing website **www.youtube.com**. Anyone can publish a video on YouTube, so the site features lots of homemade movies as well as content from major broadcasters. Whether or not you have downloaded any videos using the iTunes store, you can always watch free online films from YouTube.

● **Photos**: This app is used to watch videos you've filmed using your iPad, if you have an iPad with cameras, as you'll learn in Chapter 11.

In this section, I'll tell you more about how you can watch video on your iPad.

Using the Videos app

You will find the Videos app on your Home screen. When you start it, you can choose what type of content you want to watch (a film, TV programme, podcast, music video or iTunes U course) by tapping the appropriate button at the top. Each show is represented by its artwork or a 'still' image taken from it (see Figure 10.6). If there are too many programmes to fit in one screenful, you can drag the page up to see more.

To start viewing a programme, tap its artwork or still image. If you choose a TV show, you'll then be shown all the episodes of that show on your iPad, and you can tap a particular show to start playing it. If you tap the round Play button at the top, it will begin playing the whole series from the start.

Figure 10.6

When you tap a film's artwork, you see information about the film, which might include its summary and cast list. There's a round Play button to start the film from the beginning. If you like, you can often skip ahead to a particular 'chapter' (section) of the film. Tap the Chapters button, drag the chapters list to find the one you want and then tap it to start the film from that point.

If you tap Get More Episodes, you'll be taken into iTunes to download or buy more content from the same series, podcast or iTunes U course.

While a video is playing, you can tap the screen to show the controls. These are similar to the YouTube controls shown in Figure 10.7, which we will come to later. At the bottom, there are Back and Forward buttons, which you tap and hold to rewind or fast forward. If the video has chapters, you can tap these buttons to skip through them, as well: tap the Back button once to start from the beginning of the current chapter, and tap it again to jump to the previous chapter. Tap the Forward button to advance to the next chapter.

Between the two Back and Forward buttons is a Play/Pause button and underneath them is a slider to control the volume. You can also use the physical volume control on the side of your iPad.

At the top is a Playhead slider you can use to see how far through the programme you are, and to move through the program.

If you're watching a widescreen programme, you can double-tap the screen to change between widescreen mode (which leaves black spaces at the top and bottom of the screen) and standard mode (which chops off the sides of the image so it can fill the screen).

In the top left is a Done button, which will take you back to the Videos app, so you can choose what video you'd like to play next. Your iPad remembers how much of a TV show, film, podcast or iTunes U course you've watched, so when you come back to a programme next time, it will start playing from where you left off. To play a film from the start, choose the first chapter before playing. For a TV programme or other video without chapters, start it playing and then tap the Back button to go back to the start.

Playhead control   Download progress

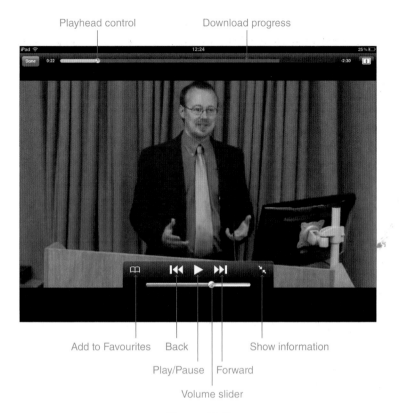

Add to Favourites   Back   Show information

Play/Pause   Forward

Volume slider

Figure 10.7

Deleting videos from your iPad

Films and TV shows take up a lot of space on your iPad, so it's a good idea to delete them from your iPad after watching them. As long as you've bought the videos or downloaded them for free, and you've kept them on your computer, you can always copy them from your computer to your iPad again to watch another time. Take care when you delete films, though: if you delete a film that you have rented, it will be permanently deleted and you'll have to pay again to get it back. If you buy videos (or anything else) using your iPad, you should make sure that you've backed them up on your computer (see Chapter 9) before you delete them from your iPad.

To delete a programme or series from your iPad, go into the Videos app so you can see all the programmes you have (as in Figure 10.6). Then tap and hold on the programme or series artwork until the Delete button (a cross in a circle) appears in the top left. Tap that and then confirm. To delete an individual episode of a TV series, tap the artwork to view the list of episodes, and then swipe your finger from left to right (or right to left) across the episode summary to reveal the Delete button. This is similar to the way you deleted emails in Chapter 5.

Watching online films from YouTube

The Videos app will work wherever you are, but you'll need an Internet connection to use the YouTube app. That's because YouTube films are downloaded from the Internet and you don't save them but watch them as they're downloading. Because the programmes aren't stored on your iPad permanently, you can happily watch YouTube until your eyes go square – unlike content you buy from the iTunes store, for which there's a limit to how much will fit in your iPad.

YouTube is free to watch, and there's a wealth of comedy, tutorial and dramatic content on there. There are full length films and programmes, but most YouTube videos are just a few minutes long, making them perfect for snacking on between other programmes.

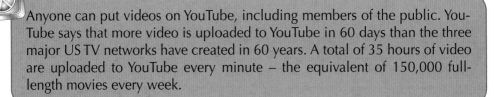

Anyone can put videos on YouTube, including members of the public. YouTube says that more video is uploaded to YouTube in 60 days than the three major US TV networks have created in 60 years. A total of 35 hours of video are uploaded to YouTube every minute – the equivalent of 150,000 full-length movies every week.

Start the YouTube app and you'll see a selection of featured videos, which you can drag up to see more. You can tap the buttons at the bottom of the screen to explore the top rated and most viewed films. There's also a button you can use to quickly find any films you've marked as your favourites.

Most of the time, though, you'll want to use the search box in the top right to find something to watch. Try entering some words relating to your hobbies or interests;

or, if you know the user name of a friend who posts content on YouTube, try entering that. The screen will fill with film suggestions. For each one, there is a still picture, the length (eg '03:44' means three minutes and 44 seconds) and how many times the video has been viewed. Tap a film and it will start to play.

As with the Videos app, the controls fade away so you can concentrate on the film, but you can bring them back by tapping the screen. Because the film has to download from the Internet, it can take a moment or two before it begins to play. The runner for the playhead control along the top of the screen fills with grey to show how much of the video has downloaded to the iPad.

Figure 10.7 shows the YouTube player in action. This short film is of me delivering a talk about Facebook and Twitter to U3A members in London last summer. Most of the controls indicated in Figure 10.7 will be familiar to you from the Videos and iPod apps. There are a few additional controls, however: you can add videos to your favourites so you can quickly find them later, and you can tap the Show Information button to see more information about the film while it plays.

When the film finishes playing, the app takes you to the information page for the film you've been viewing (see Figure 10.8). Underneath the film, you can read a summary of it, provided by the person who published the film on YouTube. Across the top of the film are buttons you can use to add it to your favourites, share the video (by email), or give a video the thumbs up, or thumbs down.

Although anyone can share films on YouTube, I've never come across anything inappropriate. If you did find objectionable or illegal content on YouTube, you could report it by tapping Flag, to flag inappropriate content to the service's owners.

You can watch films on YouTube as much as you want without having an account, but certain features are restricted to registered users. You'll need to register before you're able to tap the Like or Dislike buttons, add comments to videos or publish your own films. To get your free account, visit www. youtube.com using the Safari app (see Chapter 7) or your main computer.

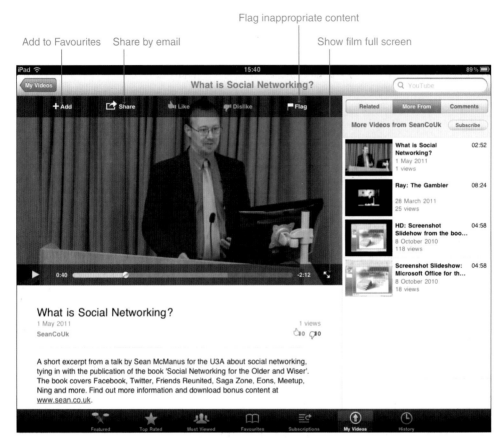

Figure 10.8

The column on the right of the information page helps you find other films to watch. If you want to see what else the same film-maker has made, tap More From at the top. If you prefer to see what others have filmed on a similar theme, tap Related.

Also on the right, the Comments button shows you comments from other viewers and gives you a chance to add your own. Any comments you enter can be read by anyone on the Internet, so take care about what information you share here.

Summary

● The iPod app is used to play audio content on your iPad.

● You can browse and play your music by Songs, Artists, Albums, Genres or Composers.

● Shuffle plays an album, playlist or other music selection in a random order.

● You can loop a list of songs or an individual song so it plays over and over again.

● You can create playlists on your iPad or on your computer.

● Smart playlists can only be created on your computer. They enable you to make a playlist by requesting songs with particular characteristics, such as a particular artist name or year of release.

● The Videos app is used to play videos downloaded from the iTunes store.

● When a video is playing, tap the screen to show the playback controls.

● You can delete videos you've watched from your iPad to free up space on it.

● The YouTube app shows you free short films on the Internet.

● Some features in the YouTube app are only available after you register at the YouTube website.

Brain training

The iPad is a fantastic entertainment device, and a great way to enjoy music, films and educational content. Refresh your knowledge of the key points in this chapter with a quick quiz.

1. The playhead control is used to:

(a) Move to a different point in a song

(b) Skip to the next track

(c) Show how much of a YouTube video has downloaded

(d) Create a playlist

2. To watch videos downloaded from the iTunes store, you use:

(a) The YouTube app

(b) The Videos app

(c) The iTunes app

(d) Any of the above

3. You tap and hold the Forward button to:

(a) Skip to the next song

(b) Skip to the next film chapter

(c) Fast forward through a song to the guitar solo

(d) Fast forward through a boring bit in a film

4. To create a smart playlist of the CDs you ripped this year:

(a) Set Year to the current year

(b) Set Date Added to between 1 January and 31 December this year

(c) Set Time to 12 months

(d) Limit to items selected by the most recently played

5. You need to register a YouTube account to:

(a) Publish your own videos on YouTube

(b) Add comments to videos

(c) Watch videos on YouTube

(d) Search videos on YouTube

Answers

Q1 – a and c   **Q2** – b   **Q3** – c and d   **Q4** – b   **Q5** – a and b

PART IV
Having Fun with Your iPad

Don't the photos of you and Mark look fantastic on this iPad! You can see every little wrinkle!

Taking and browsing photos on your iPad

Equipment needed: Any iPad, to view photos and copy them from your computer or from a digital camera. An iPad with built-in cameras, if you want to take photos with your iPad. If you want to copy photos directly from your digital camera to your iPad, you'll need the Apple Camera Connection Kit (sold separately).

Skills needed: Familiarity with starting and using apps, with using on-screen controls and with gestures including pinch and flick.

The iPad's large, high-definition screen is perfect for showing off your digital photographs to friends and family. In this chapter, I'll show you how you can add photos to your iPad from your digital camera or your computer, and how you can browse them on your iPad.

If you have a newer iPad, you can also take photos using the device. When Apple released the second generation of the iPad (the iPad 2), it introduced two cameras, one on the front of the device and one on the back. The pictures they take are lower quality than you would get from a modern digital camera, but they can be good for capturing informal shots, especially if you carry your iPad everywhere with you and don't usually travel with a camera. In Chapter 6, you learned how to use the iPad to make video calls using the cameras. In this chapter, I'll show you how to take still photos and videos.

If you want to take a picture (a screenshot) of what's on your iPad's screen, press and release the Home button and the Wake/Sleep button at the same time. It takes practice to do this without turning the iPad off!

Taking photos with your iPad

If you have a first generation iPad without cameras, skip ahead to 'copying photos between your computer and your iPad'.

It's easy to take photos with the iPad. To begin, start the Camera app. You'll be asked whether the app can use your current location. If you agree, photos and videos will be tagged (labelled) with the location where they were taken. That allows you to browse them on a map later, which is a nice alternative to a photo album or slide show.

When you use the Camera app, the screen is almost filled with a view through one of the cameras. Figure 11.1 shows the camera app in action.

If you can't recognise what's on screen, check that you don't have your finger or something else obstructing the lens, and move the iPad around to make sure that it's not pointing at a wall or ceiling.

Here's how to take a photo using your iPad:

1. Tap the Swap Cameras button in the top right to change between the front and back cameras. The back camera is higher quality than the front.

2. Frame your shot. Line up the iPad so it's pointing at what you want to photograph. Remember that if you want a photo of someone looking at the camera (including yourself, if you use the front camera), they need to look into the lens when the photo is taken, and not at the screen or back of the iPad.

3. Set the focal point. Tap the most important part of the picture, and a box will show on it (see Figure 11.1). The iPad uses this to set the focus and exposure for the picture.

4. Set the zoom. If you're using the back camera, a zoom control appears at the bottom of the screen, which you can slide from left to right to zoom in and out.

5. Tap the Take Picture button. You'll see the aperture close on screen briefly, and will hear a shutter sound unless you have muted your iPad (see Chapter 2).

Swap cameras

Review shots   Focal point   Take picture   Still/video switch

Zoom control

Figure 11.1

To view your photos, tap the Review Shots button in the bottom left, which shows a tiny version of the last picture you shot. When you tap it, it takes you to your Camera Roll album, which stores images created on the iPad, including any pictures you've saved from websites. The way you navigate this album is the same as the Photos app, which I'll show you later this chapter. There's an additional button, though: when you've finished reviewing your photos, you can tap Done in the top right to go back into the Camera app.

Shooting videos with your iPad

The Camera app can also be used to shoot high definition (HD) video. In the bottom right of the screen is a switch to choose between taking still images and shooting video (see Figure 11.1). When you slide the switch from the camera icon to the video camera icon, the Take Picture button changes to a Record button. Tap it to start filming, and tap it again when you want to stop. While you are recording, the button will flash.

This is a bit confusing: you won't be able to see any of the videos you've made while you're in the Videos app. Instead, they are kept in your photo album, so you browse and play them using the Photos app.

Using Photo Booth for special effects

The Photo Booth app, which comes with the iPad, enables you to take photos with special effects applied to them, such as x-ray, mirror effects, kaleidoscope or a simulated thermal camera. When you start the app, you can see the effects that are available on the camera. Tap one of the effects, and you go into the camera with that effect applied – for example, Figure 11.2 shows a picture of a piano taken with the simulated thermal effect.

You can use either camera to do this, by tapping the Swap Cameras button in the bottom right (see Figure 11.2). There's no focus or exposure setting in Photo Booth. If you're going to mash people's faces around or colour trees blue, there doesn't seem much point! You can adjust the non-colour effects (mirror, kaleidoscope, twirl, squeeze, light tunnel, and stretch) by pinching and/or dragging the screen. To take a picture, just point your iPad, and tap the Take Picture button at the bottom centre of the screen. To try a different effect, tap the button in the bottom left.

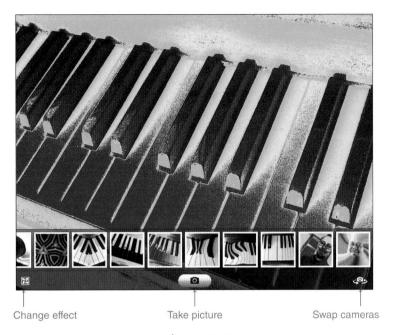

Change effect   Take picture   Swap cameras

Figure 11.2

Your photos automatically go into your Camera Roll album. At the bottom of the screen, you can see small versions of the pictures you've taken, called thumbnails. You can drag the thumbnail strip left and right to view all the pictures you've taken in Photo Booth. If you tap one, it will fill the screen. You can then tap the Delete button (a cross in a circle) on its thumbnail to get rid of it, or tap the Take Picture button to get back to taking photos.

When you view a photo, the controls disappear after a moment so you can see all of it. To bring the controls back, tap the picture.

If you want to email your creations to someone, tap one of the thumbnails, then tap the Use Photo button that appears in the bottom right corner, in place of the Swap Cameras button. You can then tap any of the thumbnails to select them (tap again to de-select), and tap Email to send them in a new email message. Who can you surprise with a weirdly warped family portrait?

Copying photos between your computer and your iPad

Whether you're an early adopter who bought the first iPad without cameras, or someone who has a more recent iPad with cameras built-in, you can copy any digital photos you have on your computer to your iPad.

Connect your iPad to your computer and start the iTunes software, then click your iPad's name on the left so you can see the synchronisation settings. Click to display the photo settings (see Figure 11.3), and tick the box beside Sync Photos to enable photos to be copied from your computer.

Next, you need to choose which photos you want to put to your iPad. Click the pulldown menu and click 'Choose folder' and you can pick which folder on your computer you want to copy photos from (see Figure 11.3). Alternatively, you can choose a program like Photoshop Elements from this pulldown menu to use photos from that program instead. I keep the photos I want to copy to my iPad in a folder called 'Current photography', but you could just copy your usual photos folder.

The folder you're copying photos from might have other folders inside it. Your My Pictures folder, for example, might have a different folder for each batch of photos you copied from your camera. By default, iTunes will copy all the folders inside your chosen folder of photos to your iPad. If you want to pick one or more of these subfolders to copy to your iPad, click the radio button beside 'Selected folders' and a list of folders will appear below. Click the tickbox beside those you wish to copy (see Figure 11.3).

When you've finished choosing photos, click the Apply button in the bottom right. Whenever you synchronise your iPad with your computer, iTunes will update your iPad so it has the same photos as your chosen folder(s).

Photos are resized for the iPad's screen, so make sure you always keep the full-size copy safe on your computer.

Choose folder to copy photos from   Show photo settings

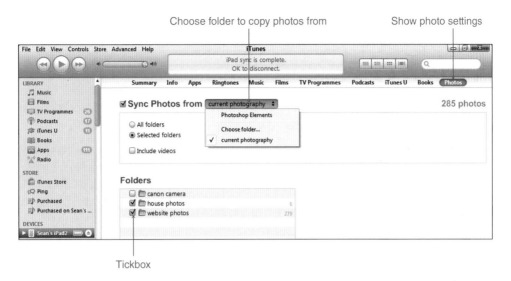

Tickbox

Figure 11.3

You can also copy photos or other images from your iPad to your computer. If you have an iPad with cameras, you can copy across photos you've taken. Otherwise, you can copy across any pictures you've made using apps, including any screenshots you've taken.

When you connect your iPad to your computer, it looks like a digital camera to your computer, even if it's an iPad without built-in cameras. If you already copy photos from your digital camera to your computer, you can use the same process to copy photos from your iPad. You can use software such as Adobe Photoshop Elements or iPhoto, for example, or in Windows you can use the Scanner and Camera Wizard (on Windows XP) or choose to Import Pictures when the Autoplay menu appears (Windows Vista and Windows 7).

If you don't have any software you can use to copy images from your iPad to your computer, you can do it manually. On a Windows PC, you can also view your iPad as if it were another disk or a USB key on your PC and then copy the images from the iPad to your computer. To do that, connect your iPad to your computer and follow these steps:

1. On your PC, click the Start button in the bottom left of the screen. (This has the Windows icon or the word 'Start' on it.)

2. Click (My) Computer.

3. You'll see a list of drives and devices that are connected to your PC. One of these should be your iPad. Double-click this, and keep browsing and double-clicking the folders until you see the photos that are on your iPad.

4. Now you've found your photos, you can copy them to your PC in the same way you copy any files. For example, click one of the photos and then hold down the Control key on the keyboard and tap A to select all photos. Hold down the Control key and tap C to copy them all. Then click where you would like them copied to (such as your desktop, or your My Pictures folder) and then use Control and V together to paste them.

You can also delete photos from your iPad using Windows on your PC. Use the preceding steps to navigate to your photos folder on your iPad, and then select and delete the photos you want to erase.

There's no recycle bin on the iPad, so when you delete a photo it is irretrievably deleted from the iPad. Make sure you have a copy on your PC first if you want to keep the photo and are just trying to free up some space on your iPad.

To copy photos from an iPad to a Mac, open iPhoto and click your iPad's name on the left. Click Import All in the bottom right, or click on the pictures you want to import and click Import Selected. If you're using an older version of iPhoto, you'll be presented with the Import pane, and will need to click the Import button to copy all your photos from your iPad to your computer.

Copying photos from your camera to your iPad

The iPad might not be your first choice for taking holiday snaps, but you can still use it to view and email photos you take with your digital camera. It doesn't matter which version of the iPad you have, but you'll need to buy a special kit from Apple that enables you to transfer files from your digital camera to your iPad.

Apple's iPad Camera Connection Kit comes with two adapters, either of which can be plugged into the socket your iPad usually uses for charging or synchronising with your computer. One of these adapters has a USB socket, so you can connect your camera to it using the cable that usually connects your camera to your computer. The other adapter takes SD cards, which most digital cameras use for storing digital photos. Both adapters are small enough to take anywhere. Each is about 4cm by 3cm by 1cm, including the transparent protective lid you'll need to remove before you can use the adapter. Figure 11.4 shows the SD card adapter in close up.

Figure 11.4

To use the digital camera adapter, you plug your camera's USB cable into your camera and the adapter, plug the adapter into your iPad and switch your camera on. To copy photos directly from your camera, you need your camera to be in its transfer mode. The way you do this varies by camera, so consult your camera's instructions or follow the prompts on your camera's screen.

Using the SD card adapter is much simpler. You just insert your SD card into the adapter and then insert the adapter into your iPad's socket.

When you connect either of these adapters to your iPad, the iPad will go into the Photos app and show you the photos on the camera or SD card, as you can see in Figure 11.5. Copying photos to your iPad is called 'importing' them. If you want to import all the photos from your camera to your iPad, tap the button to Import All at the bottom of the screen. You can also delete all the photos using the Delete All button, but take care – this will delete all the photos from your camera.

Figure 11.5

Alternatively, to select a photo, tap it and a blue tick will appear in its bottom-right corner. You can choose as many photos as you want, dragging the screen up to see more, and then tap Import to copy the selected photos to your iPad. You can also tap Delete to delete the selected photos from your camera. The Import button will give you another chance to import all the photos even if you've already selected some, as you can see in Figure 11.5.

During importing, you'll see all the blue ticks on photos turn green as the pictures are copied across. When it's finished, your iPad will ask you if you want to delete photos from your camera. Don't lose concentration here and tap Delete by mistake!

Be very careful if you choose to delete photos while using the iPad Camera Connection Kit – when you delete them, you remove them from your SD card or camera completely, and you won't be able to copy them from your camera to your computer later.

When you have finished, you can disconnect your adapter from the iPad. You can copy the photos stored on your iPad to your computer in the same way you copy images taken or created using the iPad.

Viewing photos on your iPad

Whether you take photos using your iPad, or copy them from your camera or computer, the iPad is ideal for showing them off. The Photos app is designed to do exactly that, so fire it up to get started.

As you can see in Figure 11.6, your photos are organised in several different ways. You can tap the Places button at the top to see your photos arranged on a map. This uses positioning data stored in the photo when you take a photo using an iPad. More impressively, it will also pick up place names in any descriptive tags you've added to your photos using Windows or a program like Adobe Photoshop Elements. Tap a pin on the map to see one of the photos taken there, then tap that picture to see them all.

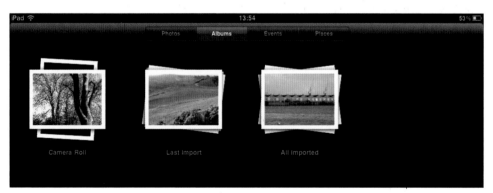

Figure 11.6

Using the Events option at the top of the screen (see Figure 11.6), you can see photos you have imported from your camera organised by date. This option doesn't appear for photos you've synchronised from your computer or photos you've taken using your iPad.

When you tap Albums, or start the application for the first time, you can see your photos organised into folders. The folders you see on your iPad will depend on what pictures you have on there and how they got there, but they might include:

- **Camera Roll:** This includes images created on your iPad, including photos you've taken using it.

- **All Imported:** This includes all the photos you have imported from your digital camera or SD card.

- **Last Import:** This album makes it easy to find the last batch of photos you imported from your camera.

- **Photo Library:** Where available, this shows you the photos you've synchronised from your computer. This only appears if you don't import photos from your camera too.

- **Folders from your computer:** If you copy photos from your computer and those photos are organised in folders, you will see those folder names too.

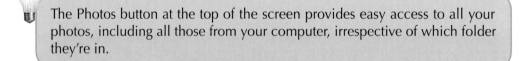

The Photos button at the top of the screen provides easy access to all your photos, including all those from your computer, irrespective of which folder they're in.

Tap an album, and thumbnails of all the photos in it will appear. Tap a photo, or use the pinch gesture to enlarge it, and it will expand to fill the screen. You can use the pinch gesture to zoom (see Chapter 7), and can drag the enlarged picture around to see different parts of it. When you rotate your iPad, the picture rotates too. If you use the iPad in the same orientation as the photo (for example, viewing a landscape shaped picture with the iPad in landscape orientation), the picture will enlarge to fill the screen.

Figure 11.7 shows the controls available to you when you're looking at a photo. They are:

- **Album browser**: See another photo in this album by touching its tiny thumbnail at the bottom of the screen. You can just roll your finger along this strip of thumbnails. You can also flick the main photo that fills the screen to the left to see the next photo, or flick right to see the previous one in the album.

- **Delete photo**: This is used to delete a photo from your iPad that you have created using the iPad or imported directly from your camera. This is not available for photos that are synchronised from your computer: to remove them from your iPad, you have to remove them from the folder on your computer that is synchronised with your iPad. Then, when you next synchronise your iPad with your computer, the photos will be removed from your iPad.

- **Rotate photo**: This is only available for photos you've imported from your camera or SD card. Tap this to rotate the photo so it's the right way up. Each time you tap, the photo revolves 90 degrees to the left. For photos that you synchronise to your iPad from your computer, you should ensure you have rotated the pictures on your computer so they are the right way up before you synchronise them to your iPad.

- **Use photo**: Tap this to email the photo, set it as your iPad wallpaper, assign it to one of your contacts (see Chapter 4), print it, or copy it so you can paste it into another app.

- **Back**: The button in the top left will take you back to the album so you can see thumbnails for all the pictures in it. In Figure 11.7, it says 'Last Import' because that's the name of the album this photo is in. You can also use a pinch (zoom out) gesture to close a photo and go back to the album. When you're looking at the album, a button in the top left takes you back to see all your albums so you can choose another one.

If you admire your photo for a moment or two, the controls will disappear so you can see it clearly. To bring them back, tap the photo. You can double-tap a point on the photo to zoom in on it and double-tap the screen again to zoom out.

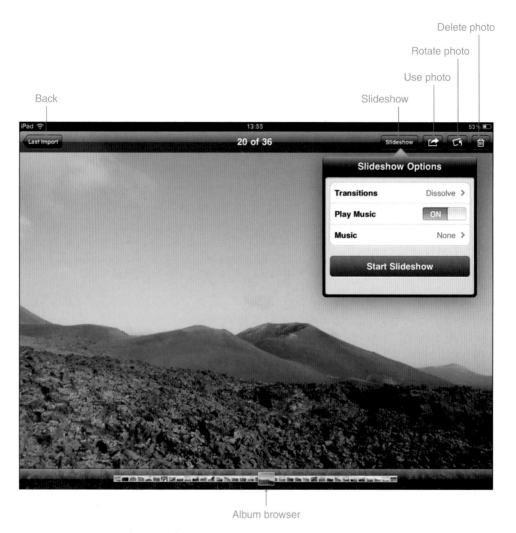

Delete photo

Rotate photo

Use photo

Back   Slideshow

Album browser

Figure 11.7

Watching a slideshow

A slideshow is a great way to enjoy your photos. You can start it running and then hand the iPad to a friend to watch, or use the iPad case to stand up your iPad so it works like a digital photo frame.

To start a slideshow featuring photos from the album you're browsing, tap the Slideshow button in the top right, indicated in Figure 11.7, and a menu opens.

A number of special effects (called transitions) are used between the photos, and you can tap to choose from several different effects. They range from the simple Dissolve, where one photo fades into another, to the elaborate Origami, where your photos are combined into collages that fold like pieces of paper.

If you have music on your iPad, you can choose a song to accompany your slideshow, by switching the Play Music switch on and then tapping Music underneath to pick a song.

Tap Start Slideshow and the slideshow will begin. You can tap the screen to stop it again.

You can change how long each slide is shown for, and whether photos repeat or appear in a random order (shuffle). Go into the Settings app, and tap Photos on the left.

The iPad also has a photo frame option, which you can use without unlocking your iPad. This works independently of slideshows in the Photos app, so to change the transition, timings and photos shown, go into the Settings app and tap Picture Frame on the left. To start the Picture Frame when your iPad is locked, instead of sliding to unlock it, tap the Picture Frame button in the bottom right (this looks like a picture of a flower).

The Picture Frame feature is set to show all photos by default, which could be a privacy threat. Because you can use Picture Frame when the iPad is locked, anyone can use the Picture Frame feature, even if your iPad is protected with a passcode. In the Settings app, you can choose to restrict the Picture Frame so that it only shows folders of photos that you don't mind anyone seeing.

Viewing videos on your iPad

If you have shot your own videos using the iPad, you will find them in your Camera Roll album in the Photos app. The videos appear as thumbnails, mixed in among your still photos. When you tap one, the first frame fills the screen; to play it, just tap the Play button in the middle of the screen or in the top left. Across the top of the screen is a control showing different frames from the film. By touching this, you can jump to different parts of the film, and then play or pause using the button in the top left.

When you tap the Use Video button in the top right (this looks the same as the Use Photo button indicated in Figure 11.7), you can email the video or upload it to video-sharing site YouTube, so anyone can see it on the Internet.

Summary

- The Camera app is used to take photos on iPads with built-in cameras.

- If you allow the camera to use your location, you can view the photos you take with your iPad on a map.

- When taking photos with the iPad, tap the most important part of the picture to focus and reveal the zoom control.

- Images and videos created using the iPad go into your Camera Roll album.

- The Photo Booth app that comes with iPads that have built-in cameras enables you to take pictures with special effects applied.

- Even if you don't have an iPad with cameras, you can use your iPad to view your photos.

- You can synchronise photos on your iPad with your computer.

- Using the Camera Connection Kit, you can copy photos from your digital camera or SD card to your iPad.

- The Photos app is used to view photos.

- The Photos app is also used to view videos you've created on the iPad.

- You can start a slideshow of photos from the Photos app, including your choice of musical accompaniment.

- The Picture Frame feature enables your iPad to work as a digital photo frame.

- The Picture Frame feature can be used without unlocking the iPad.

Brain training

Now you're an expert on browsing photos and videos with your iPad, and taking them yourself if you have an iPad with cameras, let's try a short quiz.

1. When taking a photo with the iPad, you can zoom in by:

(a) Using the pinch gesture

(b) Tapping the screen and then sliding the zoom control

(c) Using the front camera

(d) Tapping and holding the Take Picture button

2. The Camera Roll is:

(a) What happens when you rotate your iPad

(b) The album containing photos you've imported

(c) The album containing the photos you've taken or images you've made on your iPad

(d) A somewhat dry and crunchy sandwich

3. To see the videos you've shot on your iPad, you use:

(a) The Camera app

(b) The Videos app

(c) The iPod app

(d) The Photos app

4. To zoom the view of a photo you've taken, you can:

(a) Tap the photo and use the zoom control

(b) Rotate the screen so the photo fills it

(c) Use the pinch gesture to zoom in

(d) Double-tap the photo

5. To start the Picture Frame feature, you need to:

(a) Tap its icon on the Home Screen

(b) Tap the flower icon on the lock screen

(c) Tap Picture Frame in the Photos app

(d) Go into the Camera app

Answers

Q1 – b   **Q2** – c   **Q3** – d   **Q4** – b, c and d   **Q5** – b

Adding and managing apps and books

12

Equipment needed: An iPad with an Internet connection.

Skills needed: Experience using the iTunes store (see Chapter 9) is helpful but not essential. Familiarity with gesture controls is helpful (see previous chapters).

So far in this book, you've learned about the many things your iPad can do using the apps that Apple installs on your iPad for you. That's only the start of the story, though. There are thousands of programmers out there, and they're constantly coming up with new apps that allow you to use your iPad in all kinds of imaginative ways. However obscure you think your hobby is, there's bound to be an app for it among the 65,000 iPad apps currently available.

In this chapter, I'll show you how to download new apps to your iPad, how to remove them again and how to organise them. I'll also give you a few pointers to some of the best apps you might want to try out.

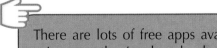

There are lots of free apps available, and many people spend more time using apps they've downloaded than the built-in apps. In some ways, this is the most important chapter in this book.

Downloading apps to your iPad

All the apps you add to your iPad, including the free ones, come through the app store, which is part of the iTunes store. When you tap the App Store icon on your Home screen, you'll see a screen that looks similar to the iTunes store for music and video (see Chapter 9).

You navigate the app store like a web page (see Chapter 7). To see more offers, drag the screen up. To jump back to the top, tap the status bar. To find out more about a particular app or offer, tap its artwork. As in the music and video store, you buy and/or download an app by tapping its Price button.

At the bottom of the screen are buttons to take you into different parts of the store (see Figure 12.1). It's worth checking what's new in the Featured section from time to time, because this shows Apple's hand-picked recommendations for the best apps. The Top Charts section shows you the most popular paid and free apps, which is another nice way to uncover some gems. You can also tap the Categories button to see apps organised by categories such as books, business, education, health and fitness, music, lifestyle, news, travel and weather.

> If you go into the Genius section, via the button at the foot of the page, the app store will recommend new apps for you based on others you've down-loaded. You first need to turn on Genius for apps, and accept the terms and conditions. This is a great way to find new apps you'll like.

You can search for apps using the search box in the top right of the screen. The search results screen has some filters across the top, so you can refine your results to focus on one category, new releases, apps with top ratings and those that are free.

There are three types of app:

● **iPhone apps**: These are apps that were designed for the iPhone and iPod Touch, which are pocket-sized devices. Their apps work fine on the iPad, too, but they only use a tiny portion of the screen. When you are using an iPhone app, you can tap the 2x button in the bottom-right to enlarge it to fill the screen, but that can make the content appear 'blocky'.

- **iPad apps**: These are designed for your iPad and will make full use of the available screen space. These are sometimes called HD apps (short for high definition).

- **Hybrid apps**: These are designed to work well on both the iPad and the iPhone, so you can use them with confidence on your iPad. If you have an iPhone or iPod Touch, you can also use the app on those devices, and it will often have a different screen layout to accommodate the smaller screen size. Hybrid apps are indicated with a tiny + in the top-left corner of the Buy/Download button.

> You can filter your search results to show only apps that are designed for the iPad. On the search results page, tap Device at the top and choose iPad. The search on the iPad also prioritises apps designed for the iPad and shows them higher up the screen.

When you find an app you like the sound of, tap its icon to see its information page, which looks like Figure 12.1. You can drag the page up to see more information, including ratings and reviews from previous customers at the bottom of the screen. You can drag the screenshot left to see more pictures, too. The description is provided by the developer, and some pages will also show information about what's new in the latest version of the app. Tap More on the right to show the description and information about what's new in full.

Some apps are free to download, but enable you to buy additional content from inside the app. These 'in-app purchases' are sometimes used to buy the latest content for a newspaper app or additional characters for a game app. Where an app enables in-app purchases, you can see a chart of the bestsellers on the left. It's worth looking out for this because you can sometimes download a free app only to find it's empty and you have to buy the content to fill it! The app's reviews will normally warn you if this is likely to happen.

> App creators sometimes release cut-down versions of their apps for free so you can try them before you buy. These are called 'lite' versions. Tap the Developer Page link in the top right of the page to see other apps by the same developer, which might include a lite version of the app you're looking at.

Buy/download   Expand description

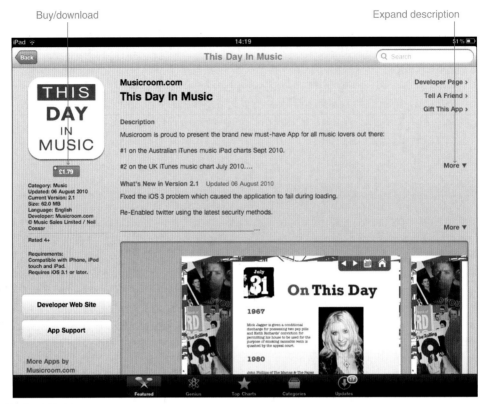

This Day in Music

Figure 12.1

To download and install an app, tap the Buy/Download button (the button underneath the app's logo that shows its price). The button will go green and then you just need to tap it again to confirm you want to install the app. If the app is a paid app, your credit card will be charged. If you're not already logged in, you'll be prompted to log in using your Apple ID, which is the same one you use for Find my iPad, music downloads and other services Apple provides.

If you haven't previously downloaded any music, video or apps to your iPad, you'll need to verify your payment information before you can proceed, even if the app is free. You'll be shown your account information, and will need to tap beside where it says 'security code' and enter the three-digit security number on the back of your credit card. When you've finished confirming your details, tap Done in the top right of the window.

Once you've confirmed the purchase or free download, the App Store will close and your app will begin to download to your Home screen. You can watch the downloading progress with a bar that goes across the app's icon, although you can also go ahead and use other apps while you wait. When the download has finished, tap the icon to start using your new app.

You can also download apps using the iTunes software on your computer (click on the left to go into the iTunes Store, and then click App Store at the top of the screen). Any apps you download to your computer can be synchronised to your iPad when you connect it.

When you run an app for the first time, you might be asked whether you want to allow push notifications. These enable the app to give you new information when you aren't using it, for example by displaying a 'new message' alert on screen or showing you how many messages you have waiting on the app's icon. It's a good idea to restrict push notifications to your favourite apps. They can run down your battery more quickly, and it can get annoying if you receive too many interruptions. You can change which apps may use notifications at any time by going into the Settings app and tapping Notifications on the left.

You might also be asked whether you will allow the app to use your location. Some apps, such as a travel app that finds restaurants near you, will need this to work properly. Others can be enhanced by location services, such as photography apps that store the location with each photo you take, so you don't have to remember it. There are privacy implications, though, because an app could, in theory, publish your location on the Internet or use it to target advertising to you (although few do). I recommend that you only give apps permission to use your location if it's necessary for the app to do what you want it to. You can change which apps can use your location by going into the Settings app and tapping Location Services on the left.

Many apps have their own settings available in the Settings app. If you can't get the app to do something you want to do, check here.

From time to time, the makers of apps update them. The App Store icon on the Home screen shows you how many updates are available for the apps you have installed on your iPad. The number is in a red circle in the top-right corner of the App Store icon. To get your updates, go into the App Store and then tap Updates at the bottom. Updates are usually free, and bring new features to the app. Occasionally, app creators remove features from their apps, too, so read the version information and reviews to make sure the update won't cut off a feature you like.

You can have up to 11 Home screens of apps. The Home screen indicator at the bottom of the screen (see Figure 12.2) shows you how many screens there are (each screen is represented by a dot) and which one you're viewing (the dot that is coloured white). To move between the Home screens, flick left and right. This is the same way you brought up the Spotlight search in Chapter 3.

If you're in a Home screen or the Spotlight search, you can press the Home button to go to the first Home screen.

Rearranging your apps and web clips

In this section, I'll show you how to organise the apps on your Home screens, but the same ideas apply to web clips (web page bookmarks that you've added to your Home screen, see Chapter 7).

To rearrange the icons on your iPad, go to a Home screen, and tap and hold one of the icons. All the icons will start to jiggle around, which means you're in the mode for arranging icons, as shown in Figure 12.2. Touch an icon and keep your finger on it and it will enlarge. Without lifting your finger, move it across the screen and the app icon will go with it. Move your app to a space near another app and keep it there, and that app will jump out of the way to make room. When you release your finger, your app will drop into that space.

Apps aren't like folders on your desktop computer, which you can put anywhere on the screen, because you can't have empty spaces between apps. Apps are always arranged in rows starting at the top of the screen. You can't add an app to the second row until the first one is filled. If you want to drop an app into the last available space, move the icon across the screen and hold it in the empty space for a moment before lifting your finger. The app will bounce into the next space, just after the last app on the screen.

The shelf at the bottom of the screen is called the 'dock'. The dock has the same icons on every Home screen. There is room for six apps or folders on the dock and you can move the default apps (Safari, Mail, Photos, iPod) to a normal Home screen to make room for your own apps on the dock. When the dock is full, if you want to add a new app to the dock, you need to move one of the apps from there to the Home screen above to make room.

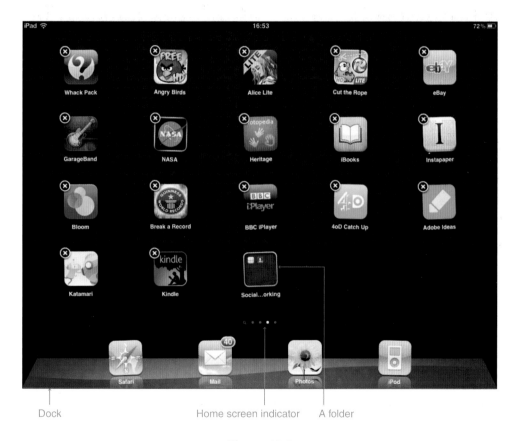

Dock   Home screen indicator   A folder

Figure 12.2

If you put an app directly on top of another app and then release your finger, a new folder is created and opened containing both apps, shown in Figure 12.3. All the other app icons fade into the background, so just the apps inside the folder can be seen clearly. You can enter a name for the folder, rearrange the apps inside it, and leave the folder again by tapping outside of it. To add new apps to the folder, move them onto the folder's icon, hold for a moment and then release your finger. To remove apps from the folder or change its name, tap it when you are in arrangement mode. You can then edit the name box or drag the icons from the folder into the greyed out parts of the Home screen to lift them out of the folder. To delete a folder, simply remove all the items from it. Once you've finished viewing a folder, just tap outside it to go back to the Home screen. Each folder can hold up to 20 apps.

Figure 12.3

Moving apps to a different Home screen is a tricky manoeuvre. You need to move an icon to the right or left edge of the screen and then hold it there a moment until the next Home screen rolls into view. If you go too far and move off the screen, the app will bounce back into place and you'll have to start again.

To stop arranging icons, press the Home button. The apps will stop jiggling and you can now start apps by tapping their icons in the usual way. To start an app that's inside a folder, first tap the folder to open it and then tap the app's icon.

As you've probably noticed by now, when you rotate your iPad, the apps change their position on the screen. In portrait mode, you have five rows of four apps, and in landscape mode, you have four rows of five apps. The apps are arranged in the same sequence in both modes, filling the rows from the top left, but the different lengths of the rows mean that many of your apps will move to a different position on the screen when your rotate the iPad.

Deleting apps and web clips

When you are in arrangement mode, all the apps and web clips you've added to your iPad have an X in the top-left corner. To delete a web clip, tap this X and then confirm you want to delete it. (You can't delete web clips using the iTunes software on your computer.)

If you tap the X in the top-left corner of an app's icon, it will ask you to confirm you want to delete it, before deleting the app and all its data from the iPad. To make sure you can install the app again later, I recommend removing apps using the iTunes software on your computer instead, as explained in the next section.

Changing the apps on your iPad using your computer

When you connect your iPad to your computer, any apps you have downloaded using the app store on your iPad will be copied to your computer, together with any data in those apps. If you have a problem with your iPad, you can restore it to its factory settings and copy across the information from this backup to recover your iPad (see 'Troubleshooting and fixing your iPad' in Chapter 2).

You can use the iTunes software on your computer to choose which apps are on your iPad, too. Connect your iPad to your computer, start the iTunes software and follow these steps, referring to Figure 12.4.

1. On your computer, in the iTunes software, click your iPad's name on the left.

2. Click the Apps category at the top of the screen.

3. On the left of the main panel, use the Sort by Kind menu to choose how you want to browse your apps (by category, date or name).

4. A list of the apps you have on your iPad will appear on the left. Tick the box beside any apps you'd like on your iPad. Untick the box beside any apps you don't want on your iPad. You can install them again later if you want to.

5. On the right, you can arrange where each app appears on your Home screens. You use the large picture of a Home screen to arrange icons, and the smaller pictures underneath it to choose between Home screens. Click a small Home screen picture to choose that Home screen and you'll see its apps in the large Home screen picture. If you want to change an app's position on the screen,

click it, hold down the mouse button, drag the app to the space where you want it and then release the mouse button. The other icons will rearrange themselves to make room. To move an app to a different Home screen, click its icon and drag it in a similar way onto the small Home screen box underneath. To start a new Home screen, drag your icon onto the greyed-out box to the right of your choice of Home screens.

6. To make a folder containing apps, use your mouse to drag one app directly on top of another app. Enter a name for the folder when prompted. To move apps out of a folder again, double-click the folder and drag the apps back on to the Home screen, outside of the folder.

7. Click the Apply button in the bottom right.

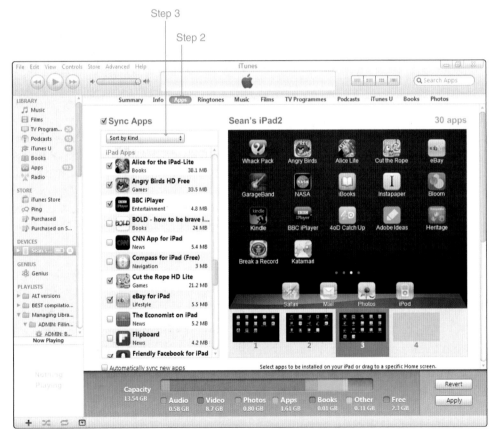

Figure 12.4

Underneath the panel showing the apps, you have a tickbox to automatically sync new apps. If you tick this, any apps you buy on your computer will automatically be copied to your iPad when you synchronise your iPad with your computer.

Multitasking with apps on your iPad

When you quit an app by pressing the Home button, the iPad keeps a record of the state the app was in when you did that. This means you should see the same documents and information on screen when you return to the app.

Don't rely on this to permanently store your data. If you've got important information in an app, use whatever mechanisms are provided by the app to save it.

There is a quick way to switch between different apps you've recently used. If you press the Home button twice quickly, the Home screen fades out and the Recents list pops up from the bottom of the screen underneath the dock, showing the icons for the apps you used most recently, as you can see in Figure 12.5. Tap one of these icons to go back into it, or flick the bar to the left to see more apps. If you don't want to use one of these apps, tap in the faded-out area or press the Home button to return to your normal Home screen.

You can remove apps from the Recents list if you want to. Press the Home button twice to show the list, then tap and hold one of the icons. They will all start to jiggle around. Tap the minus sign in the top left corner of an icon and it will be removed from the list. To finish, tap outside the Recents list or press the Home button.

Flick the Recents list to the right and you can call up brightness, volume and iPod app playback controls. There's also a button in the bottom left of this panel to lock the screen orientation. Normally the screen contents adapt to which way up you hold your iPad, but locking the screen orientation stops this.

Figure 12.5

Reading books on your iPad with iBooks

If you're an avid reader, one of the first apps you'll want to install is iBooks, Apple's app for downloading and reading books on your iPad. Apple will prompt you at various times to download iBooks (including when you first enter the app store), but you can download it at any time by searching for it in the app store. The app itself is free, but you'll have to pay to download many of the books. Classic works of literature are often available for free download because they're out of copyright.

When you first start the app, it will ask if you want to sync your bookmarks, notes and collections between devices. If you plan to use iBooks on a number of different devices, this helps you to keep all your information synchronised across them. Otherwise, tap Don't Sync. You can change this in the Settings app later if you need to.

When the app starts, you'll see an empty bookshelf. To download your first books, tap Store in the top-left of the screen and you'll enter the book store, which looks and feels the same as the app store. As with apps and music, you tap the Price button to buy a book (or download it for free). To get a free sample, tap the Get Sample button. When you've finished browsing the store, tap Library in the top left to return to your bookshelf.

To start reading a book, tap its cover in your library on your bookshelf. You can read books in portrait (where the pictures might be larger) or landscape orientation (which feels more like a real book).

You can double-tap a picture to enlarge it and then use the pinch gesture on it to zoom in further. When you've finished, tap the picture and then tap Done in the top right.

To turn to the next page, put your finger on the right of the screen and flick it left. To go back a page, put your finger on the left of the screen and flick it right. You can also slide the page chooser along the bottom of the screen.

Figure 12.6 shows iBooks in action, with its controls labelled.

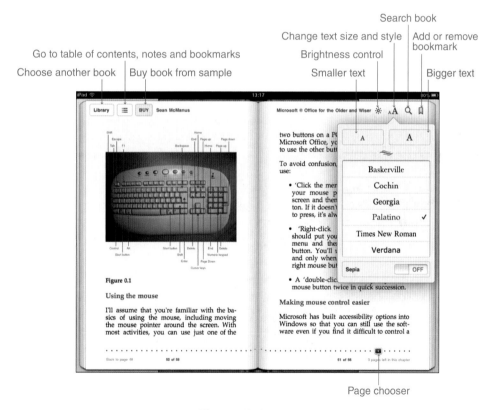

Figure 12.6

There's some clever stuff you can do with a digital book (ebook) that you can't do with a real book. Tap and hold on a word, for example, and you can look it up in the dictionary or search the rest of the book for the same word.

You also have the option to add a note to the page. Unlike when you scribble comments in the margin of a printed book, you can quickly see all your notes in one place by going to the bookmarks page for your ebook (see Figure 12.6). When you're reading a book, the notes appear in the margin. Just tap them to enlarge them, and tap outside them to hide them again.

If you struggle to read small print, you can change the text size. Just tap where indicated in Figure 12.6 to open your options for text size and style. Then tap the Bigger Text button until you can read comfortably.

Books can include links, too. For example, if you tap an entry in the table of contents, you'll jump to the relevant section of the book. You can also tap a website link to open its web page in Safari.

Alaska Airlines has ditched the heavy airline manuals pilots used to carry around in favour of the iPad. Instead of carrying 11 kg of paper onto the plane, each pilot has a company-issued iPad with 41 flight, systems and performance manuals on it.

20 more apps to get you started

Part of the fun of the iPad is exploring the store to find the apps that are perfect for you – the apps on someone's iPad are as much an indicator of their personality as the books they own. But to get you started, here are some suggestions for apps you might want to take a look at. Many of these are free at the time of writing, but prices and specifications change from time to time, so check the store for the latest information.

- **4oD Catch Up**: Channel 4's app for watching TV shows you might have missed.
- **Alice for the iPad**: Alice in Wonderland with a difference – this 'next generation' pop-up book uses sophisticated physics modelling to make the illustrations interactive. There's a free lite version you can try out first.

- **Angry Birds HD**: An odd game, but an addictive one, in which you catapult the birds to knock down the pigs' houses. Over 100 million copies of Angry Birds have been downloaded across lots of different devices, and there is a free edition available.

- **BBC iPlayer**: Brings selected BBC TV and radio programmes to your iPad.

- **Bloom**: An app co-created by ambient musician Brian Eno. It creates relaxing music based on where you tap the screen, and the music evolves and changes endlessly.

- **Cut the Rope**: An addictive puzzle game with cute graphics for the iPad. Try the free lite version first, which includes a tutorial.

- **eBay**: Browse, bid and buy in eBay's online auctions.

- **Flipboard**: Gathers information from various online publications and from Facebook and Twitter (if you use them) and presents it like a magazine. Turn the pages to browse the news that matters to you.

- **Fotopedia Heritage**: 25,000 photographs of all UNESCO World Heritage Sites.

- **GarageBand**: Apple's simple music studio enables you to play an onscreen keyboard, drum kit, guitar and sampler.

- **Guardian Eyewitness**: Every day, a new high-quality reportage photo is downloaded to your iPad, together with a photography tip.

- **Guinness World Records**: An entertaining cut-down version of the famous book, tailored for the iPad, with sections dedicated to the fastest, tallest, craziest, strangest, most expensive and deadliest.

- **iMovie**: Apple's app for creating and editing high-definition videos on your iPad, including themes and transitions to give your video a professional look.

- **Kindle**: Amazon's app for downloading and reading books on your iPad that you have bought from the Kindle store at **www.amazon.co.uk**. If you have a Kindle ebook reader, you can read the same books on your iPad without paying twice.

- **NASA App HD**: Browse NASA's library of videos, photos and articles, and find out about current and past missions.

- **New York Times**: Read the newspaper in your iPad. The top news section is free, and other sections are subscription-based. Many other newspapers and magazines have apps, too, so it's worth checking whether your favourite does.

- **Shazam**: An app that identifies music that's playing. Handy if you miss the DJ's introduction when you're listening to the radio or you want to identify a song that's being used in a TV show.

- **TED**: Free videos of inspiring talks from the TED conference, which is dedicated to ideas worth sharing. The conference began in 1984 with a focus on technology, entertainment and design (hence the name TED), but its scope is much broader now. The event takes place twice a year, but you can check in any time with this app.

- **Tesco Recipes**: A free recipe book with more than a thousand recipes, integrated with online shopping so you can easily order the ingredients you need.

- **Trip Advisor**: A handy app for your holidays. Find restaurants, hotels, and tourist attractions near you and read reviews from other travellers.

If you're a keen gamer, tap the Game Center icon on your Home screen to find games that you can play against your friends over the Internet.

You can find links to these apps in the section of my website devoted to this book at **www.sean.co.uk**.

Summary

- You can enhance your iPad with free and paid apps.

- All apps are downloaded from the app store, using the App Store app on your iPad or iTunes software on your computer.

- Your iPad can run iPhone apps too, but they only use a small portion of the screen.

- To download an app on your iPad, tap its price in the store.

- Free updates for your apps are available in the app store, too.

- Push notifications enable apps to give you an alert even when the app isn't running.

- Tap and hold an icon on your Home screen to go into arrangement mode.

- In arrangement mode, you can rearrange your app icons or create folders for your apps.

- You can have up to 11 Home screens of apps.

- Apps on the dock are always visible on screen, whichever Home screen you are viewing.

- Apps downloaded on your iPad are backed up on your computer when you connect to it.

- Using iTunes on your computer, you can change which apps are on your iPad at any time.

- To see recently used apps, press the Home button twice quickly.

- The best app on the iPad is whatever turns out to be your favourite. Everyone's different, so explore the store!

Brain training

Are you app happy, or appsolutely confused? Try this quick quiz to refresh the key points in this chapter.

1. The 2x button is used to:

   (a) Download an app again

   (b) See the apps you recently used

   (c) Enlarge an iPhone app to fill the screen

   (d) Cheat by making two moves in the Noughts and Crosses app

2. Pressing the Home button twice quickly will:

   (a) Go into arrangement mode

   (b) Take you to the Spotlight Search

   (c) Show you recently used apps

   (d) Provide quick access to lock the screen orientation

3. If you drag one app on top of another app in arrangement mode:

   (a) Your iPad creates a new folder containing both apps

   (b) Other apps jump out of the way to make room for the app you're dragging

   (c) The apps swap places

   (d) The app you're dragging jumps to the next free space

4. You can use the iTunes software on your computer to:

   (a) Download apps

   (b) Change the apps on your iPad

   (c) Rearrange the layout of apps on your iPad

   (d) See the apps you used most recently

5. To download an app from the app store on your iPad:

   (a) Tap its artwork

   (b) Tap its name

   (c) Tap its price

   (d) Tap 'More'

Answers

Q1 – c   **Q2** – c and d   **Q3** – a   **Q4** – a, b and c   **Q5** – c

Glossary

3G A mobile Internet connection that works in a similar way to a mobile phone connection. You need to pay a subscription to use 3G and have a 3G signal available wherever you are when you want to use it. The signal is available most places in urban areas, most of the time. Not all iPads support 3G.

app Short for 'application', this is a program on your iPad, such as Notes or Mail. The iPad comes with many built-in apps and you can download additional paid and free apps from the app store.

app store Apple's app store enables you to download new apps for your iPad, many of which are free. You can access it through the App Store icon on your iPad's home screen or by using the iTunes software on your computer.

Apple ID You use your personal Apple ID to access various services provided by Apple, including FaceTime, Find my iPad, the iTunes store for buying music and video, and the app store. Your ID is a combination of your email address and a password you set up when you first create your Apple ID.

bookmark Bookmarks are used to keep a note of web pages, ebook pages or map locations you might want to refer back to later.

Contacts The Contacts app provides a single place to store information about your friends, which is then shared with the Mail, Maps and FaceTime apps. This ensures those apps have postal addresses, phone numbers and email addresses available to use whenever they're needed.

dock The dock is the shelf at the bottom of the Home screen showing several apps. The dock's apps are the same on all your Home screens, so it's used to make sure you can always quickly find the most important apps. A dock is also a device you can buy for propping up your iPad while it is connected to your computer or for connecting it to a keyboard.

double-tap To briefly touch something on the screen twice in quick succession.

drag A gesture used to scroll around the screen so you can see different content on it. Touch the screen and move your finger up, down, left or right. It is used, for example, if a web page spills off the bottom of the screen and you need to drag the web page up to see more.

FaceTime Apple's app for video conferencing. This is only provided on iPads that have built-in cameras.

flick A gesture for quickly moving through content. Touch the screen and move your finger left, right, up or down quickly, lifting your finger part-way through.

gestures Ways to control the iPad by touching its screen in different ways, such as by briefly touching an icon (tapping it) or by moving your fingers closer together or further apart while they're on the screen's surface (the pinch gesture).

high definition (HD) A term for high quality video. Also sometimes used to indicate apps that are designed for the iPad's large screen.

Home button The round button on the front of the iPad. Press it to exit apps and return to the Home screen.

Home screens The screens full of app icons that enable you to choose which app you'd like to use next.

icon A small picture used to represent an app on the Home screen. Tap an app's icon to start the app.

iPhone Apple's mobile phone, which also runs apps but has a much smaller screen than the iPad. You can use iPhone apps on your iPad, but they only use a small part of the screen by default and can become 'blocky' when you enlarge them.

iPod The iPod app on your iPad is used to play music and other audio content. Apple also makes a range of music players called iPods, including the iPod Touch, which can run apps but has a much smaller screen than the iPad.

iTunes This word is commonly used to refer to two different things. The iTunes software runs on your computer and is used to manage your iPad and the content on it. The iTunes store is used to buy and download music, video and other content. It is accessed on your iPad by tapping the iTunes icon on the Home screen. You can also access the iTunes store on your computer using the iTunes software.

iTunes U Short for iTunes University, this provides free educational programmes for download from the iTunes store.

landscape When you use your iPad in landscape orientation it means it is wider than it is tall, like a painting of a landscape.

lock When your iPad is locked, the screen is off and it doesn't respond to your touch. It can continue to play music. To unlock the iPad, press the Home button and slide the onscreen switch. Alternatively, open your iPad's smart cover if it has one.

pinch A gesture used for enlarging content on screen (zooming in) or reducing its size (zooming out). Put two fingers on the screen and move them further apart to zoom in. Close your fingers together to zoom out again.

portrait When you use your iPad in portrait orientation it means it is taller than it is wide, like a portrait painting.

Sleep/Wake button This is the button on your iPad that is used to lock your iPad or switch it off. If you hold your iPad with the round Home button at the bottom, the Sleep/Wake button is in the top right corner.

Spotlight search The search built into the iPad that can be used to find notes, emails, contacts, videos and audio content stored on your iPad.

status bar The black bar across the top of the iPad's screen, which shows the time and the status of the battery and Internet connection. In many apps, you can tap the status bar to jump to the top of the page content.

synchronising When you connect your iPad to your computer, content is copied between them both. Your contacts and web browser bookmarks, for example, will be synchronised (synched) so the same information is stored on both your iPad and your computer. You can also choose which audio, video, podcasts, photos and other content are copied from your computer to your iPad. Any content you create or download on your iPad is automatically backed up to your computer when you connect to it.

tap A gesture where you briefly touch something on the screen (or tap it). It is used to start apps by tapping their icons, to select content by tapping its summary (in Notes or Mail), and to press buttons on the screen.

tap and hold A gesture where you touch something on the screen and keep your finger on it. You tap and hold an image or a link in the web browser to open additional options, and tap and hold an app icon on the Home screen to enter arrangement mode, for example.

touchscreen The screen on the iPad. It not only displays information but also recognises where and when you touch it, so that you can control the iPad.

unlock When your iPad is locked, it does not respond to your touch and the screen is off. To unlock your iPad, press the Home button and slide the slider to the right.

wallpaper The image that appears behind your icons on your Home screens. You can change your wallpaper in the Settings app.

web browser The program used to view and interact with web pages. On the iPad, this is the Safari app.

web clip A bookmark for a web page, which appears on your Home screen like an app icon.

Wi-Fi A wireless Internet connection that you can use on your iPad to access the Internet, the app store and the iTunes music and video store. You can set up your own Wi-Fi at home, and it is also often provided at cafés, holiday resorts, and hotels. Wi-Fi only works in a relatively small area, around the Wi-Fi hotspot.

YouTube A website that anyone can use to publish and view videos. On your iPad, the YouTube app enables you to search and view videos from the YouTube website.

Index

B

C

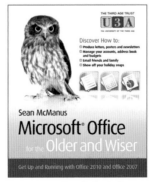